Muhammad Ali

" I Am the Greatest "

Read about other
American REBELS

Andy Warhol
"Everyone Will be Famous for 15 Minutes"

ISBN-13: 978-0-7660-3385-6

Elvis Presley
"I Want to Entertain People"

ISBN-13: 978-0-7660-3382-5

James Dean
"Dream As If You'll Live Forever"

ISBN-10: 0-7660-2537-3

Jimi Hendrix
"Kiss The Sky"

ISBN-10: 0-7660-2449-0

John Lennon
"Imagine"

ISBN-13: 978-0-7660-3675-8

Johnny Cash
"The Man in Black"

ISBN-13: 978-0-7660-3386-3

Kurt Cobain
"Oh Well, Whatever, Nevermind"

ISBN-10: 0-7660-2426-1

Madonna
"Express Yourself"

ISBN-10: 0-7660-2442-3

Malcolm X
"I Believe in the Brotherhood of Man, All Men"

ISBN-13: 978-0-7660-3384-9

Muhammad Ali

" I Am the Greatest "

John Micklos, Jr.

Enslow Publishers, Inc.
40 Industrial Road
Box 398
Berkeley Heights, NJ 07922
USA

http://www.enslow.com

Library of Congress Cataloging-in-Publication Data

Micklos, John.
    Muhammad Ali : "I am the greatest" / John Micklos, Jr.
        p. cm. — (American rebels)
    Includes bibliographical references and index.
    Summary: "A biography of boxing legend Muhammad Ali, discussing his early struggles with racism, rise to fame as a world heavyweight champion, personal hardships, including his refusal to be drafted during the Vietnam War, and legacy"—Provided by publisher.
    ISBN 978-0-7660-3381-8
    1. Ali, Muhammad, 1942–   —Juvenile literature. 2. Boxers (Sports)—United States—Biography—Juvenile literature. I. Title.
    GV1132.A4M54 2010
    796.83092—dc22
    [B]   2009017593

Printed in the United States of America

052010 Lake Book Manufacturing, Inc., Melrose Park, IL

10 9 8 7 6 5 4 3 2 1

To Our Readers: This book has not been authorized by Muhammad Ali or his successors.

We have done our best to make sure all Internet Addresses in this book were active and appropriate when we went to press. However, the author and the publisher have no control over and assume no liability for the material available on those Internet sites or on other Web sites they may link to. Any comments or suggestions can be sent by e-mail to comments@enslow.com or to the address on the back cover.

Every effort has been made to locate all copyright holders of material used in this book. If any errors or omissions have occurred, corrections will be made in future editions of this book.

♻ Enslow Publishers, Inc., is committed to printing our books on recycled paper. The paper in every book contains 10% to 30% post-consumer waste (PCW). The cover board on the outside of each book contains 100% PCW. Our goal is to do our part to help young people and the environment too!

Illustration Credits: Associated Press, pp. 6, 9, 17, 29, 35, 40, 46, 58, 73, 90, 95, 108, 121, 127, 134; Christian Burris, p. 87; © Columbia/courtesy Everett Collection, p. 125; Everett Collection, pp. 22, 100; Getty Images, p. 52; Library of Congress, p. 12; Sports Illustrated/Getty Images, p. 83; Time & Life Pictures/Getty Images, p. 116; © Topham/The Image Works, p. 70.

Cover Illustration: Sporting Pictures/Rex Features/Courtesy Everett Collection.

Contents

Muhammad Ali stands outside the Houston federal courthouse in April 1967.

Chapter 1

Taking a Stand

"I refuse to be inducted into the armed forces of the United States because I claim to be exempt as a minister of the religion of Islam."[1]

That simple statement, made on April 28, 1967, changed forever the life of twenty-five-year-old Muhammad Ali. That day, he went from being simply the heavyweight boxing champion of the world to being a rebel, taking on the mighty United States government. His protest against serving in the Vietnam War came at a time when most of the American public still supported the nation's involvement there.

The United States wanted to prevent the pro-American government of South Vietnam from being taken over by the communist regime that ruled North Vietnam. By 1967, some four hundred thousand American troops were already stationed in Vietnam. And now Ali was refusing to join them.

Ali already served as a lightning rod for controversy.

Many people admired his wit and flamboyant style. Others despised him for what they perceived as arrogance. His conversion to the Muslim religion in 1964, when he changed his name from Cassius Clay to Muhammad Ali, caused further controversy.

During the Civil Rights Movement in the 1960s, the United States struggled with how to fully and equally integrate African Americans into the nation's economic, political, and social structure. Meanwhile, the Nation of Islam—or Black Muslims as they were also called—believed in opposing white oppression by whatever means necessary, including violence. This frightened many whites. It also disturbed some African-American leaders, including the Reverend Dr. Martin Luther King, Jr., who advocated nonviolent action to gain equal rights for blacks.

Ali's refusal to be drafted caused a tidal wave of reaction. Not only was he one of the most famous people in the United States, but his stand also had political, racial, and religious undertones. It led to nationwide discussion of all of these issues.

For refusing to enter the U.S. Army, Ali was sentenced to five years in prison and fined ten thousand dollars. He remained free while his lawyers appealed the case. However, he was stripped of his heavyweight title. States revoked his boxing license. His passport was confiscated. This prevented him from boxing anywhere in the world.

Ali did not fight for three and a half years. Those years, when he was in his late twenties, mark the prime

Ali is surrounded by the press in Houston in 1967.

of most fighters' careers. "We never saw him at his peak," his trainer, Angelo Dundee, said years later. "If he'd continued getting better at the rate he was going, God only knows how great he would have been."[2]

Ali lost millions of dollars in potential earnings during this period. He did not waste time feeling sorry for himself, though. He kept busy on various projects. He toured college campuses, where he "talked, orated, rapped, and preached his way around Islam, black pride, love, hate, integration vs. segregation, boxing, economics, and any number of his views on life."[3] He also performed in a Broadway play.

A remarkable thing happened while his case worked its way through the courts. As casualties mounted in Vietnam, the tide of public opinion gradually began to turn against the war. Many people who had at first disagreed with Ali's refusal to be drafted now supported him. They applauded him for risking his career and his fortune to speak out against what more and more people were coming to believe was an unjust war. "During his exile," wrote biographer Thomas Hauser, "Muhammad Ali grew larger than sports. He became a political and social force."[4]

Finally, on June 28, 1971, more than four years after Ali had refused to be inducted into the army, the U.S. Supreme Court unanimously voted to reverse his conviction. This further raised his status as a hero for many people. Ali was much more modest, saying, "I never thought of myself as great when I refused to go into the Army. All I did was stand up for what I believed."[5]

Ali's passion to speak his mind and stand up for his beliefs stood as a hallmark throughout a boxing career that spanned more than twenty years. Long after he retired, he continued to tour the world promoting peace and spreading goodwill even as his own health deteriorated.

Decades after his boxing career ended, Muhammad Ali remained one of the best-known and most beloved figures in the world. Over the years, he truly earned the nickname he first bestowed upon himself way back in 1964 when he first won the heavyweight crown: "The Greatest."

Chapter 2

It Began With a Bike

"Whites Only." "No Coloreds Allowed." Signs such as this were common throughout Louisville, Kentucky, in the early 1940s. Like many cities in the southern United States in those days, Louisville was segregated by race. Blacks lived in one section of town. Whites lived in another. They rarely interacted on a personal level. Blacks could only drink from certain water fountains. They could only use certain restrooms. They were denied access to many restaurants.

Meanwhile, World War II had raged throughout much of the world since 1939. The United States entered the conflict following the Japanese attack on the naval base at Pearl Harbor, Hawaii, on December 7, 1941. The fighting continued until Germany and Japan surrendered in 1945.

This was the world into which Cassius Marcellus Clay, Jr., was born on January 17, 1942. His name, like his father's, paid tribute to General Cassius Marcellus

In the United States, in the 1940s, much of American society was segregated. In many places, African Americans could not drink from the same water fountains as white people.

Clay, a noted abolitionist from Kentucky who spoke out to abolish slavery in the nineteenth century. His father, Cassius, Sr., was a sign painter. His mother, Odessa, added to the family's income by cleaning and cooking for white households across town. Both of his parents were keenly aware of political and racial issues.

The war ended when Cassius was three, so it did not really affect him. The segregation and discrimination he experienced while growing up, however, shaped many of the beliefs he carried throughout his life. It bothered him, even as a young child, to see that blacks were not allowed into many stores and offices. "What did they do with the colored people?" he would ask his mother.[1] At the time, most people used the terms "colored" or "Negro" to refer to black people. The term African American did not come into use until much later.

His mother recalled, that "We called Muhammad 'GG' when he was born because—you know how babies jabber at the side of their crib—he used to say 'gee, gee, gee, gee.'"[2] Years later, he joked that he was trying to say Golden Gloves.

According to his mother, Cassius walked and talked early. He was never still, and he walked on tiptoes all the time. When his younger brother, Rudolph, was born, Cassius acted as the protective big brother. If his mother tried to spank Rudolph, Cassius would grab him and say, "Don't you hit my baby."[3]

Cassius called his mother Mama Bird. He recalled that on Sunday mornings, his mother would wake up his brother and him and make them a nice breakfast. While they ate, she ironed their best clothes. Then the boys took a bath, got dressed, and got ready for Sunday school. "I can remember trying hard not to get dirty," he said. "I knew I looked handsome in my freshly ironed shirt and bow tie."[4]

Odessa Clay made sure the boys went to church every Sunday. She taught them to treat everyone kindly and not to be prejudiced against anyone. Years later, Muhammad Ali said this about his mother: "She's a sweet, fat, wonderful woman, who loves to cook, eat, make clothes, and be with family. She doesn't drink, smoke, meddle in other people's business, or bother anyone, and there's no one who's been better to me in my whole life."[5]

Around the neighborhood, Cassius played marbles and touch football. He was great at touch football, recalled his brother, because he was so fast that no one could tag him. He didn't like tackle football because he thought it was too rough.

But Cassius did do one thing that might seem dangerous. It might even seem foolish. He asked Rudy to throw rocks at him. "He thought I was crazy, but no matter how many he threw, he could never hit me," Cassius said. "I was too fast. I was running left, and right, ducking, dodging, and jumping out of the way."[6] Years later, he would put those evasive maneuvers to good use in the boxing ring.

Although Cassius Clay, Sr., painted signs for a living, he also considered himself an artist. He painted murals as well as signs. When his sons were old enough, he took them along on jobs and taught them how to paint. "Before he started fighting, Muhammad could lay out a sign," his father recalled. "Draw the letters, do the spacing, mix the paint, and fill it in right."[7]

In some ways, the Clays were a close, loving family, but they faced their share of troubles, too. Cassius Clay, Sr., sometimes drank too much and became violent. On three occasions, his wife called the police for protection. Over the years, he was arrested several times on charges such as reckless driving, disorderly conduct, disposing of mortgaged property, and assault and battery. But he proudly noted that he never spent one night in jail.[8]

Cassius Clay, Sr., also sometimes saw other women. This greatly angered his wife and years later led to their divorce.

It bothered him, even as a young child, to see that blacks were not allowed into many stores and offices.

In 1954, at age twelve, Cassius had an experience that changed the course of his life. He had received a new red-and-white Schwinn bike. It was his first new bike, and he was very proud of it. One day in October, he and a friend rode to the Louisville Home Show, a bazaar ran by black merchants. There they browsed the exhibits and enjoyed the free food.

When Cassius went outside after the event, his red-and-white Schwinn bike had vanished. Someone had stolen it. Cassius was very upset. His family could not afford to replace the bike. He also feared getting in trouble for losing it.

Cassius looked for a police officer so that he could report the theft. People told him there was a policeman at the Columbia Gym nearby. Officer Joe Martin ran a boxing club there. Martin later recalled the event this way: "One night this kid came downstairs, and he was crying. Somebody had stolen his new bicycle. . . . He was only twelve years old then, and he was gonna whup whoever stole it. And I brought up the subject, I said, 'Well, you better learn how to fight before you start challenging people that you're gonna whup.'"[9]

From that moment on, young Cassius was hooked on boxing. He spent all his spare time training. "I was the first one in the gym, and the last to leave. I trained six days a week."[10]

"My bike got stolen and I started boxing, and it was like God telling me that boxing was my responsibility," he later said. "God made us all, but some of us are made special. . . . Some people have special resources inside, and when God blesses you to have more than others, you have a responsibility to use it right."[11]

After just six weeks of training, eighty-nine-pound Cassius made his boxing debut. Before the fight, Cassius was nervous. The boy he was fighting was a little older and a little bigger. But Cassius's father walked by his side as he made his way down the aisle to the ring. He assured young Cassius that he would do fine. And he did, winning a three-round split decision over another novice fighter named Ronnie O'Keefe.

Did Martin know then he had hooked up with a person who would one day become one of the greatest

In 1954, twelve-year-old Cassius Clay is ready for his amateur ring debut.

heavyweight boxers of all time? Hardly. "I guess I've taught a thousand boys to box, or at least tried to teach them," Martin later recalled. "Cassius Clay, when he first began coming around, looked no better or worse than the majority."[12]

Within a year, however, Martin noticed that Cassius had a lot of potential. He already had the speed that would later become his trademark. He also possessed plenty of determination. "He was a kid willing to make the sacrifices necessary to achieve something worthwhile in sports," Martin said. "I realized it was almost impossible to discourage him. He was easily the hardest worker of any kid I ever taught."[13]

After just six weeks of training, eighty-nine-pound Cassius made his boxing debut.

He was also one of the biggest eaters. His voracious appetite helped him grow from a skinny kid into a heavyweight. His family recalled that one Christmas he devoured an entire duck in addition to his share of the traditional turkey. And Martin noted that "he would eat enough food for three or four other boys."[14]

Early on, Cassius hoped to make a living through boxing. "When I started boxing, all I really wanted was someday to buy my mother and father a house and own a nice big car for myself," he later recalled.[15]

In school, he would pretend that the loudspeaker system was announcing him as heavyweight champion of the world. Other times he drew a picture of a jacket on a piece of paper, labeling it National Golden Gloves Champion or World Heavyweight Champion.

Still, his path wasn't easy. One day an amateur named Willy Moran knocked Cassius out cold. But it didn't bother Cassius. The next day he was back working with Moran again.

Clay also showed at an early age the smart mouth that would later earn him the nickname "the Louisville Lip." "Almost from my first fights, I'd mouth off to anybody who would listen about what I was going to do to whoever I was going to fight," he said. "People would go out of their way to come and see, hoping I would get beat."[16]

Of all his amateur battles, Cassius perhaps was proudest of the time he challenged a local bully named Corky Baker to meet him in the ring. Cassius bobbed and jabbed while Corky soon tired himself out throwing big punches that hit nothing but air. Corky quit after the second round, one eye black and his nose bloody. After that fight, Corky stopped picking on people. Later, Cassius recalled, "he told me that I was a good fighter and that I was going to go a long way. Then he shook my hand and walked off."[17]

While Cassius excelled in the ring, he struggled at school. Years later he realized that he had dyslexia, a condition that causes people to have difficulty reading. Often it causes them to see certain letters reversed. But at that time he did not know about dyslexia. He just knew that reading was hard.

Cassius also did not understand how to solve math

problems. He dropped out of Central High School in March 1958, but he reenrolled that September. He barely managed to graduate in June 1960. He earned an overall average grade of 72.7 between ninth and twelfth grade (70 was passing). He ranked 376th out of a graduating class of 391.

Indeed, some of Cassius's teachers thought he should not graduate at all. Principal Atwood Wilson stood up for him, however. "One day our greatest claim to fame is going to be that we knew Cassius Clay or taught him," Wilson said. "He's not going to fail in my school. I'm going to say 'I taught him!'"[18]

Part of the problem was that he was acutely aware of the prejudice against blacks throughout American society. Like many others—both black and white alike—he was outraged when he learned about the 1955 murder of Emmett Till, a fourteen-year-old black youth from Chicago. Till was beaten and murdered in a small town in Mississippi because he had allegedly flirted with a white woman in town. An all-white jury found the two men arrested for the crime not guilty. Most observers deemed the trial a farce.

The incident made Cassius realize the odds he faced in trying to succeed in a world controlled by whites. He saw black people with high school diplomas and college degrees hanging out on street corners because they could not find not jobs. Many blacks did not even complete high school. They dropped out before that point because they saw little hope through education.

"I started boxing because I thought this was the

fastest way for a black person to make it in this country," he said. "A boxer can just go into a gym, jump around, turn professional, win a fight, get a break, and he is in the ring. If he's good enough he makes more money than ballplayers make all their lives."[19]

By this time, Cassius was devoting himself almost exclusively to boxing. He fought more than one hundred times as an amateur, losing only a handful of times. Along the way, he won two Golden Gloves championships and two national Amateur Athletic Union (AAU) titles.

One of his opponents was Jimmy Ellis. They split two close fights and became friends. "Ali spent all his time in the gym," Ellis said. "That's where he lived. He wanted to box and he wanted to be great, and that's what his life was all about."[20]

"I started boxing because I thought this was the fastest way for a black person to make it in this country."

The first time amateur referee and judge Bob Surkein saw Cassius, he realized right away that the young man had remarkable reflexes. He also realized that Cassius had a remarkable ego. One time, he and Cassius stayed at the same hotel during a tournament. Cassius had won his first tournament fight on a knockout. The next morning Surkein found that all the newspapers in the hotel's coffee shop were missing the sports section. He soon found the cause—Cassius was up in his room with a pair of scissors, cutting out pictures of himself.[21]

In 1960, Cassius won the Olympic trials in the light

Cassius Clay (center) with his teammates Skeeter McClure (left) and Eddie Crook (right) with their gold medals in 1960.

heavyweight division. This gave him the chance to travel to Rome, Italy, to participate in the Olympics. Cassius looked forward to proving himself against boxers from around the world.

Expectations were high for Cassius Clay. *Sports Illustrated* said he had the best chance of any American for a gold medal in boxing. The magazine also referred to what would become his signature footwork in the ring, saying, "Clay likes to display supreme confidence by doing intricate dance steps between passages of boxing."[22]

One major obstacle stood between Cassius and glory. He feared flying. After a rough flight going to the Olympic trials, he vowed never to fly again. Joe Martin later recalled taking him for a long walk in Louisville to calm him down. Cassius also recalled his father's advice to always confront the things he feared. He also realized that if he didn't fly to Rome, he couldn't reach his goal of winning the Olympic gold medal.

"If I had not faced that fear and gone on to win the gold medal at the Olympics, I might not have become the heavyweight champion of the world," Cassius Clay later said. "If I let fear stand in my way, I would never have accomplished anything important in my life."[23]

In the end, Cassius boarded a plane for Rome, ready to showcase his skills on the world's biggest amateur stage.

Chapter 3

The Golden Boy Turns Pro

On the flight to Italy in August 1960, Clay wore a parachute he bought at an army surplus store. He thought it might save him if the plane went down. Once in Rome, he soon established himself as the "young clown prince of world athletes." He joked with other athletes from around the world, shaking hands and telling stories.[1]

"One of my teammates told me that if I had been running for mayor of the Olympic Village, I would have won the election," Clay later recalled.[2]

Clay had such fun mingling with the other athletes in Rome that his coaches were concerned he might lose his focus. Evenings found him dancing or visiting with other athletes. One afternoon, he entertained a group by playing harmonica. Often, he spent time being interviewed by reporters. Still, Clay trained hard. He ran two miles early each morning. He worked out in the afternoon.

"He worked for that gold medal," said teammate Wilbert "Skeeter" McClure. "You don't slough off and play games when you're trying to become an Olympic champion. And certainly, when I watched him train, he was one of the hardest trainers I'd ever seen."[3]

To reach the gold-medal bout, Clay had to win three other fights, which he did—two by decision and one by knockout. Clay fought Zbigniew Pietrzykowski for the light heavyweight title. The Polish fighter, a three-time European champion, had far more experience than Clay. The first two rounds were close. In the third and final round, Clay pummeled his opponent with combinations of punches. "Ripping into the stamina-lacking Pole, he drew blood and came preciously close to scoring a knock-out," recalled British journalist John Cottrell.[4]

By the end of the bout, even the Italian fans, who had been rooting for the Polish fighter, were on Clay's side. Clay won a unanimous decision. After the bout, he stood solemnly on the medal stand that had been placed in the ring and accepted his gold medal. By the next morning, however, he was much more relaxed. He paraded around the Olympic Village, wearing the medal.

A Russian reporter asked Clay how it felt to win a gold medal for a country that wouldn't allow him to eat in many restaurants. Clay replied, "You tell your readers we got qualified people workin' on that, and I ain't too worried about the outcome. The USA is still the best country in the world."[5]

Winning the Olympic gold marked a fitting culmination to Clay's amateur career. "That was my last amateur fight," he announced after the bout. "I'm turning pro."[6]

Clay seemed ideally suited to become a popular professional boxer. At the time, most boxers were perceived as being dull and brutish. Clay, meanwhile, was handsome and entertaining.

A large crowd gathered for Clay's triumphant return to Louisville after the Olympics. There he recited the first of the many poems he would later become famous for. In this poem, he described how he triumphed in Rome just like Cassius from the days of the Roman Empire.[7]

Despite being an Olympic hero, Clay still faced the prejudices of the time. In "the best country in the world," he still couldn't eat in some places. One day he and a friend went into a restaurant in downtown Louisville. When they tried to order lunch, the waitress informed them that the restaurant did not serve Negroes. Clay had his gold medal draped around his neck. He politely explained that he was an Olympic champion. The waitress checked with her manager, but said the two still had to leave.

"I wanted to tell them all that they should be ashamed," Clay later recalled. "I wanted to tell them that this was supposed to be the land of the free. As I got up and walked out of that restaurant, I didn't say anything, but I was thinking that I just wanted America to be America. I had won the gold medal for America, but I still couldn't eat in this restaurant in my hometown."[8]

In his autobiography, *The Greatest*, published in 1975, Ali described another instance of prejudice. This one led to an often-repeated legend. According to the story, he threw his gold medal off a bridge into the Ohio River after being threatened by a white motorcycle gang. Supposedly, he was so disgusted by this incident of racial hatred that he no longer felt proud of what the medal represented. Therefore, he threw it away.

Most people, however, believe that the story is just that—a story. They believe the medal was simply lost at some point over the years. They think he uses the story to make his point about prejudice. Throughout his boxing career and beyond, he continued to speak out against racism and prejudice.

The next big step for Clay in turning pro was finding the right people to manage his career and promote his fights. Several people wanted the job, including William Reynolds, a wealthy man from Louisville. Reynolds offered Clay a ten-thousand-dollar signing bonus and a guaranteed annual income for ten years. He also wanted to let Joe Martin continue to act as Clay's trainer.[9]

At this point, Clay's father stepped in. He did not think Martin had enough experience to train a professional champion fighter. "I was aware that, without the right backing, he wouldn't have much success," Clay's father said, "so it was very important to me that he get off in the right hands. And that's what happened. I got him a good contract with people that could promote him."[10]

"I'm turning pro."

Initially, Clay was managed by the Louisville Sponsoring Group, a group of eleven wealthy white men. Together, they pooled about thirty thousand dollars to launch Clay's career. Clay received a ten-thousand-dollar signing bonus and a guaranteed salary of $333 per month, which would be deducted from his earnings. Earnings would be split 50/50 for the first four years and 60/40 in Clay's favor after that. The investors would cover expenses such as training (including a trainer's salary), travel, and promotion. Fifteen percent of Clay's income would be placed in a pension fund.[11]

Clay used some of his signing bonus to buy a used Cadillac for his parents. He also set aside some money to pay taxes.[12]

On October 29, 1960, just three days after signing the contract, Clay had his first professional fight. It took place in Louisville's Freedom Hall. His opponent was Tunney Hunsaker, the police chief of Fayetteville, West Virginia. Hunsaker boxed in his spare time and had a record of 17-8. Clay won an easy six-round decision.

Hunsaker said Clay was "fast as lightning, and he could hit from any position without getting hit." After the fight, Hunsaker predicted that the young man would one day be heavyweight champion of the world. Looking back, he said, "I'm honored, highly honored, to have been the first person Muhammad Ali fought in his professional career."[13]

Years later, Clay repaid the compliment. He sent Hunsaker an autographed photo. It said, "You gave me

Cassius Clay lands a punch to Tunney Hunsaker during their October 1960 bout.

my first fight as a professional. Thank you and may God always bless you."[14]

Soon after his first fight, Bill Faversham of the Louisville Sponsoring Group sent Clay to California to train with Archie Moore. He thought the young boxer needed more professional training. Moore was a highly respected boxer. Indeed, at the time he held the light-heavyweight championship of the world. Moore called his camp the Salt Mine. That showed how difficult the training was—like working in a salt mine. Clay trained

29

hard. He ran up and down steep hills and worked out in the gym.

Moore tried to teach Clay to punch more effectively. He tried to teach him how to fight up close. But Clay didn't always listen. He had great confidence in his abilities. "He thought he would never have to do any in-fighting because he was gonna be so swift and always out of range, etc.," Moore later recalled. "It was useless arguing with him."[15]

Clay also had to do chores at the Salt Mine. Sometimes he had to help with the cooking and cleaning. He didn't like that. After only three weeks, both teacher and student agreed it would be best if Clay went back home to Louisville. "To tell you the truth, the boy needed a good spanking," Moore later said, "but I wasn't sure who could give it to him."[16]

The Louisville Sponsoring Group searched for a new trainer for Clay. In December 1960, they went to Miami, Florida, to interview Angelo Dundee. Dundee trained a number of fighters, including Willie Pastrano, who would later win the light heavyweight crown. They offered Dundee a choice of a guaranteed salary of $125 a week or 10 percent of Clay's earnings. Unsure of Clay's potential, Dundee took the salary, which he later realized "wasn't the smartest move I've made in my life." Indeed, it could have cost him a fortune over the years. Fortunately, he and Clay's sponsors later worked out a percentage deal.[17]

Dundee suggested that Clay move to Miami after Christmas to begin training with him. The eager Clay couldn't wait. He left for Miami right away. He began training with Dundee on December 19, 1960. The two would work together for twenty years.

Clay had awesome physical gifts, which Dundee helped him to hone. Clay stood 6' 3" and had very long arms. In most fights, he had a reach advantage over his opponent. He also had blindingly fast hands and amazing footwork. He used these gifts to dance around the other fighter, peppering him with stinging jabs. When his foe tried to retaliate, he would simply dance back out of reach or bob his head. Eventually, most of his opponents grew frustrated. Then they got careless as they tried to chase after him. That gave Clay even more openings to land bigger punches.

He had blindingly fast hands and amazing footwork.

Dundee knew that simply giving Clay instructions wouldn't work. Yelling at him wouldn't work. Instead, Dundee used a mixture of flattery and encouragement. "I'm not his boss," Dundee said. "We're a team. We work together and I know how to work with him."[18]

Dundee's strategy was to let Clay think everything was his idea. If Dundee wanted him to jab more, he would say, "Gee, your jab is really coming along. You're getting your left knee into it and really stopping him in his tracks." Sometimes, that might not have been the case at all. Clay would soon be doing things the way Dundee wanted, but he would think it was all his own idea.[19]

Clay later put it this way: "Angelo Dundee was with me from my second professional fight. And no matter what happened after that, he was always my friend. . . . He was there when I needed him, and he always treated me with respect."[20]

Just eight days after he arrived in Miami, Clay had his second professional fight. He beat Herb Siler in the fourth round. Clay stopped Siler with a right to the body and a left hook to the jaw.

In early 1961, Clay won three fights in just over a month. On January 17, his nineteenth birthday, he beat Tony Esperti in three rounds. He scored a technical knockout because Esperti's left eye was badly cut. A knockout happens when a fighter is knocked down and cannot get up by the count of ten. A technical knockout (TKO) happens when the referee, fight doctor, or the boxer's handlers determine that he is unable to continue. In his next fight, Clay knocked out Jim Robinson in just two minutes.

In early 1961, Clay won three fights in just over a month.

On February 21, Clay fought in his first main-event bout against Donnie Fleeman. Fleeman, a boxer who had won forty-five fights. He proved no match for Clay. The referee stopped the fight in the seventh round.

In April, Clay was back in Louisville, battling Lamar Clark, a boxer who had knocked out his last forty-five opponents. He predicted that he would knock out Clay, too. Clay made his own prediction. He promised that

Clark would fall in just two rounds. Clay broke Clark's nose and knocked him down three times, scoring a second-round knockout. Thus began Clay's habit of predicting in which round he would win a fight. "I said he would fall in two and he did," Clay said. "I'll continue this approach to prove I'm great."[21]

Many people already thought Clay was brash. Later that year, however, he met someone whose self-promotion was even wilder. Before a fight in Las Vegas, Clay met professional wrestler Gorgeous George, who was also in town for a match. They appeared on a radio show together. Clay went first, describing how he planned to win his bout. Gorgeous George came next. He ranted about how he was going to annihilate his opponent. He promised to cut off all his long blond hair if he lost.

Clay went to the wrestling match, where he watched George put on a show as he crushed his opponent. In the locker room after the bout, George told Clay, "A lot of people will pay to see someone shut your mouth. So keep on bragging, keep on sassing, and always be outrageous."[22]

Clay built a new routine based on what he learned from George. Many people found Clay's banter refreshing. Others found it annoying. Even Angelo Dundee sometimes grew weary of his fighter's bluster. "There is only one Cassius Clay," Dundee once said. "Thank God."[23]

The media couldn't decide what to make of the brash young fighter. Some found him a breath of fresh air in a sport where many champions seemed dull. Others thought he was unprofessional. But love him or hate him, the media couldn't ignore him.

To further promote himself, Clay told photographer Neil Leifer from *Life* magazine that he trained underwater. He had never really done that, but the photographer believed him. The next morning Clay did a training session in a pool. Some of the photos ended up as a feature in *Life*. Leifer later recalled that the magazine's editors were convinced Clay really did train underwater. "Now that's a genius you don't see in people very often," Leifer said. "Genius and a bit of a con man, too."[24]

Throughout the rest of 1961, Clay continued to win bouts. His reputation continued to grow. Still, Clay had not yet battled a top fighter. Then, on February 10, 1962, he had a chance to fight contender Sonny Banks in the legendary Madison Square Garden in New York City. Fighting in the Garden brought Clay's career to a whole new audience. Clay delighted the New York media with his wit, earning nicknames such as "The Mighty Mouth" and "The Louisville Lip."

Clay predicted that Banks would fall in four rounds. In the third round, Clay was clowning around, his hands at his sides rather than guarding his head. Suddenly, Banks caught him with a left hand to the jaw. Down went Clay, much to the delight of the crowd. Clay bounced back up and finished the round. In the fourth round, Clay came out strong, knocking out Banks.

Clay announced that he would knock out opponent Archie Moore in four rounds.

"I told you," he gloated to reporters. "The man fell in four!"[25]

Over the next few months, Clay won four more fights, all by knockout or TKO. On November 15, he had the chance to fight his former teacher, the forty-eight-year-old Archie Moore. Moore did not want to fight. "I had to fight him for financial reasons," Moore said.[26]

Clay boldly predicted that he would knock Moore out in just four rounds. Then he went out and did it. Although Moore was well past his prime, people still respected him. By beating Moore, Clay gained more respect.

Clay delighted the New York media with his wit, earning nicknames such as "The Mighty Mouth" and "The Louisville Lip."

Throughout 1963, Clay kept moving up the heavyweight ranks. First he knocked out Charles Powell. He predicted a fourth-round knockout against Doug Jones, but ended up winning a decision after a lackluster fight.

Next, Clay traveled to London to battle British heavyweight Henry Cooper. British fight fans treated Clay like royalty. In the first three rounds, Clay danced around the slower Cooper, peppering him with punches and opening a large cut over his left eye. Then, in the fourth round, Cooper caught Clay flush on the jaw with a huge left hook. Clay fell back against the ropes and then collapsed to the canvas. He staggered to his feet, his legs rubbery. Then the bell rang, ending the round. Clay had to be helped back to his corner.

Dundee knew his dazed fighter had only the one-minute break between rounds to recover. Could he do it? Here came one of the turning points in Clay's career. A loss would have severely set back his plan to fight for the championship. But Dundee came up with a trick to gain his fighter precious extra time to recover.

Earlier, Clay's glove had been split. Dundee tugged at the split to make it bigger. Then he called the referee over. There was a delay as they searched for a replacement glove. That gave Clay more time to recover. "I don't know how much time that got us," Dundee later said. "Maybe a minute, but it was enough."[27]

Recovered, Clay roared out for the next round. He pummeled Cooper with heavy punches. Blood poured from the cut over Cooper's left eye. Before the round ended, the referee stopped the bout. Clay had survived a difficult fight and remained undefeated. Now he demanded that he be given a chance to battle Sonny Liston for the heavyweight championship of the world.

Chapter 4

The Greatest!

Sonny Liston. The name sent shivers down the spines of most fighters. He was big. He was tough. He was mean. He possessed one of the hardest punches in the history of heavyweight boxing.

As a teenager, Liston spent time in prison for his role in several robberies. There his boxing talent was discovered by a Roman Catholic priest, and his skill helped earn him an early parole. After a brief amateur career, he turned pro in 1953. Even as Liston's boxing career moved forward, however, he had trouble staying out of trouble. Mobsters recruited him as an enforcer. "At any sign of trouble they'd send Sonny out and maybe he'd stare a guy down or just break his leg," said one of his friends from prison.[1]

In 1956 Liston was jailed again, this time for beating up a police officer. After his release in early 1958, he resumed his boxing career. By 1960 he was a top contender for the heavyweight crown.

In September 1962, Liston fought Floyd Patterson, the reigning champion, for the title. Most people were rooting for Patterson, but Liston knocked him out in the first round. A rematch in July 1963 ended with the same result—Liston winning on a first-round knockout.

Clay attended the second Liston-Patterson fight. When it ended, he climbed into the ring and grabbed the microphone. "Liston is a tramp; I'm the champ," he yelled. "I want that big ugly bear. . . . If I can't whip that bum, I'll leave the country."[2]

After that, a reporter asked Liston how long it would take him to beat Clay in a fight. "Two rounds," Liston responded. "One and a half to catch him, and a half round to lick him."[3]

Clay kept lobbying for a title shot. He even drove from Chicago to Liston's house in Denver. He called the local media. Then he stood on Liston's lawn and taunted him. Liston came out, furious. "But before he could make up his mind what to do, the police came and told us to leave or we'd be arrested for disturbing the peace," Clay later said.[4]

Finally, in November a contract for the fight was signed. The fight was scheduled for February 25, 1964, in Miami, Florida. Most experts believed that Liston would whip Clay. Some even worried about the young fighter's safety. Sometimes, boxers have died or sustained severe brain damage from taking too many blows in the ring.

Attorney Sol Silverman of California had become a boxing investigator after the death of former featherweight

LISTON		CLAY
31	AGE	23
212	WEIGHT	210
	HEIGHT	
6 ft. 1 in.		6 ft. 3 in.
	REACH	
84 in.		79 in.
	CHEST NORMAL	
44 in.		43 in
	CHEST EXPANDED	
46 ½ in.		45 in.
	WAIST	
33 in.		34 in.
	FOREARM	
14 ½ in.		13 ½ in.
	FIST	
15 ½ in.		13 in.
	NECK	
17 ½ in.		17 ¾ in.
	BICEPS	
17 ½ in.		16 in.

This chart shows the statistics of Sonny Liston and Cassius Clay before their 1964 fight.

Davey Moore from injuries he sustained in a bout. Silverman said, "The proposed Cassius Clay-Sonny Liston heavyweight title fight is a dangerous mismatch which could result in grave injury to the young challenger. Besides, not one former heavyweight champion among the eleven now living regards Clay as being ready for Liston."[5]

Even Clay's backers did not think he was ready to take on Liston. Bill Faversham of the Louisville Sponsoring Group said, "I felt that Cassius could do with at least another year's experience before he fought Liston."[6]

"Everyone predicted that Sonny Liston would destroy me," Clay later recalled. "But it's lack of faith that makes people afraid of meeting challenges, and I believed in myself."[7]

Clay trained hard, and he studied Liston's style. He also started running his mouth. "I figured Liston would get so mad that, when the fight came, he'd try to kill me and forget everything he knew about boxing."[8]

Clay even composed a poem titled "Song of Myself," predicting his victory over the champion. In it, he said that the ringside observers would witness "the launching of a human satellite" and "a total eclipse of the Sonny!"[9]

Liston, for his part, at least pretended that Clay's banter did not bother him. He said his left fist would do his talking for him. "It's gonna go so far down his throat, it'll take a week for me to pull it out again," Liston said. Hype for the fight was building.[10]

Then something happened that threatened cancellation of the bout. Word spread that members of the Nation of Islam were spending time in Clay's training camp. Many viewed the group, also called the Black Muslims, as radical. The fight promoters feared that people would refuse to come to the fight if the Black Muslims were there.

The early and mid-1960s marked the height of the Civil Rights movement in the United States. Leaders such as the Reverend Martin Luther King, Jr., led nonviolent marches to demand equal rights for African Americans.

On August 28, 1963, King delivered his famous "I Have a Dream" speech in Washington, D.C., to more than two hundred thousand civil rights supporters. In that speech, he spoke of his hopes for a future in which blacks and whites would live together in harmony as equals. "I have a dream," King said, "that my four little children will one day live in a nation where they will not be judged by the color of their skin but by the content of their character."[11]

King called on Americans to "let freedom ring" for all across the nation. "When we let it ring from every village and every hamlet, from every state and every city," he concluded, "we will be able to speed up that day when all of God's children, black men and white men, Jews and Gentiles, Protestants and Catholics, will be able to join hands and sing in the words of the old Negro spiritual: 'Free at last! Free at last! Thank God Almighty, we are free at last!'"[12]

Not everyone shared King's vision of nonviolent change. The Nation of Islam, led by Elijah Muhammad, believed in opposing white oppression by whatever means necessary, including violence. They backed the notion of separatism. They wished to see blacks create their own communities and perhaps even their own nation.

The message of asserting the rights of black people that the Nation of Islam preached struck a chord with Clay. He had become interested in Islam as early as 1961, and over time he began to accept more and more of the religion's teachings. Still, he kept his interest quiet, fearing that if people thought he was involved with the Nation of Islam it would prevent him from getting a shot at the heavyweight title.

> **"Everyone predicted that Sonny Liston would destroy me."**

The assassination of President John F. Kennedy in November 1963 caused problems within the Nation of Islam. Kennedy was a strong supporter of civil rights. Still, Malcolm X, one of Elijah Muhammad's disciples, proclaimed that the Kennedy assassination was a case of "chickens coming home to roost." He meant that Kennedy had failed to stop the violence, which had rebounded on him.[13]

Later Malcolm X would come to change his views about white people, but in November 1963 a nation in mourning did not appreciate his comments. Elijah Muhammad feared that such remarks would hurt the Nation of Islam movement. He ordered Malcolm X not to speak in public for ninety days. The incident marked the beginning of a major split within the Nation of Islam.

In September 1963, Clay had been spotted at a Nation of Islam rally in Philadelphia. His appearance there drew little comment. But in January, he spoke at another rally in New York City, and his involvement drew news coverage. When Bill MacDonald, who was promoting the fight, learned of this, he threatened to cancel the bout. He asked Clay to deny that he was affiliated with the group. Clay refused.

To make matters even worse in MacDonald's eyes, Clay had invited Malcolm X to Miami while he trained. Clay and Malcolm X had become close friends. "In time, Malcolm became my spiritual adviser," Clay later said. "When I was getting ready for the title fight against Sonny Liston, Malcolm was especially supportive. . . . Malcolm helped me focus on my strengths, and he strengthened my belief in myself."[14]

Still, Malcolm X's presence threatened the future of the fight. MacDonald asked Harold Conrad, who was handling the details of the fight, if he could help. Conrad went to Malcolm X. "Listen, if you don't get outta town your boy's gonna blow the title shot, the promoter's gonna blow the fight and we're all gonna blow the money," Conrad said. "The smart thing is to get out and come back for the fight." Malcolm X agreed to leave town and come back for the fight.[15]

Meanwhile, hype for the bout increased. About a week before the fight, Clay met the Beatles, who were in Miami to perform on *The Ed Sullivan Show* as part of their first visit to America. Clay was late, and the Beatles grew restless. But then Clay burst through the door and greeted them warmly. The Beatles and Clay, who would become two of the biggest pop culture icons of the 1960s, took an immediate liking to each other. They clowned around together, with the Beatles even climbing into the ring, where Clay ordered them to "get down, you little worms." They even posed for a photo in which Clay appeared to be knocking all of them out with a single punch.[16]

At the weigh-in before the fight, Clay acted like a crazy man. With friend Bundini Brown and former heavyweight champion Sugar Ray Robinson at his side, Clay made a dramatic entrance. "Float like a butterfly, sting like a bee!" he shouted. Then he lunged as if to attack the champion. Liston looked at him, confused. He wondered if the challenger was really crazy.[17]

The doctor at the weigh-in found that Clay's pulse rate was 120 beats per minute, more than twice his normal rate. His blood pressure was 200 over 100, an alarmingly high rate. The doctor wondered whether the fight should go on as scheduled. Jimmy Cannon, a noted sportswriter, asked the doctor whether the physical symptoms meant that Clay was scared. "Yes, yes, Mr. Cannon," the doctor said. "This fighter is scared to death, and if his blood pressure is the same at fight time, it's all off." He instructed Dr. Ferdie Pacheco, Clay's fight doctor, to keep checking the pressure throughout the day.[18]

Clay insisted that it was all carefully planned, designed to throw Liston off his game. "The truth of the matter is I've rehearsed and planned every move I make that day," Clay said. Indeed, he was so relaxed after the weigh-in that he took a nap.[19]

Despite all the hype, the fight was nowhere near a sellout. Many fans stayed away, thinking the fight would be a mismatch. However, many people across the country did get to watch the fight on closed-circuit television. This meant that they paid to watch the fight broadcast on a screen at a movie theater or other venue. Little did they realize that they were about to witness a historic bout.

Before his own fight that evening, Clay had the chance to watch his younger brother, Rudy, make his

Clay throws a punch to Liston's face during their February 1964 bout. Clay went on to win and became the world heavyweight champion.

debut as a professional boxer. Rudy won a unanimous decision, but Cassius did not like to see the punches he absorbed. After the fight, Cassius told Rudy, "You're through fighting. I'm going to be The Champ tonight. You're not going to have to fight any more."[20] It took quite some time for Rudy to heed his older brother's advice.

In the final moments before going out to meet Liston, Clay seemed wary. His water bottles for the fight were taped shut. He asked Rudy to watch them. Then he found out that Rudy had left them alone for a few minutes. He had the bottles untaped, emptied, refilled, and retaped.

Clay feared that someone would try to drug him to make him lose the fight. He did not even fully trust his own trainer, Angelo Dundee, or his fight doctor, Ferdie Pacheco. He later revealed that he had received threatening calls before the fight. He did not trust anyone outside of his brother and his Muslim friends. "The only thing that could hurt me, I thought, was something coming through the water," he said.[21]

The fight itself was nearly as bizarre as the weigh-in. In the early rounds, Clay danced around the slower Liston, peppering him with sharp jabs that opened a cut under the champion's left eye.

At the end of the fourth round, Clay came back to the corner, and his eyes were burning. He couldn't see. Over the years, there have been many theories about what happened. One is that Liston's handlers put something on Liston's gloves to temporarily blind Clay.

When he hit Clay or the two tied up in a clinch, the substance got on Clay's head and dripped into his eyes as he sweated. Another theory is that Liston was using a liniment for his sore shoulder, and it got into Clay's eyes during the clinches. A third theory says that the substance came from the ointment that Liston's cornermen used to stop the bleeding under his eye. No one will ever know for sure.

Dundee used the minute between rounds frantically trying to clear out Clay's eyes by sponging them with water. It didn't help. Clay instructed Dundee to cut his gloves off to stop the fight. How could he possibly fight when he could barely see his opponent?

At the age of twenty-two, Muhammad Ali was heavyweight boxing champion of the world.

This single moment marked a turning point in Clay's career. If he didn't go out for the next round, if he quit, no matter how good the reason, it might be years before he got another shot at the title. "This is for the heavyweight championship; no one walks away from that," Dundee told him. "Get in there and run until your eyes clear up."[22]

And so it was that Clay lurched out into the ring for the fifth round. Indeed, he barely made it. After the fight, referee Barney Felix told reporters, "He was lucky. If Clay hadn't moved in a split second—I mean one second—he'd have been finished. I would have been forced to disqualify him."[23]

Meanwhile, behind Clay's corner, the Black Muslims at ringside were angry. They didn't trust white people. They thought Dundee had put something in his fighter's eyes to make him lose. Dundee wiped his own eyes with the sponge to prove there was only water on it.

As the round began, Clay could see only the blurred image of Liston. He used his long arms to keep Liston from getting too close. Realizing Clay could not see, Liston pushed forward. He swung heavy punches at the challenger's head and body. A few hit their mark, but most missed. By the end of the round Clay's vision had cleared, and he resumed popping jabs at the champion.

Clay dominated the sixth round. He realized Liston was discouraged and worn out. He hit the champion with jabs, hooks, and uppercuts. Back on his stool in between rounds, Liston spit out his mouthpiece. He had had enough. He quit. He later claimed that his sore shoulder prevented him from punching effectively.

Clay immediately sprang to his feet, his arms raised over his head in victory. "I am the greatest!" he shouted to the throng of reporters. "I shook up the world! . . . I'm the king of the world. . . . Eat your words!" he told those who had doubted him.[24]

At the age of twenty-two, Muhammad Ali had reached his goal. He was heavyweight boxing champion of the world. He was the greatest.

Chapter 5

The Legend Grows

Most Americans didn't know what to make of the new champion. Some found him charming and funny. Others thought he was brash and arrogant. But as his new religion became more widely known, public opinion turned firmly against him.

Two days after the fight, Clay made his religious views clear at a press conference. "Black Muslims is a press word," he said. "It's not a legitimate name. The real name is Islam. That means peace. Islam is a religion and there are 750 million people all over the world who believe in it, and I'm one of them."[1]

Then, on March 6, 1964, Elijah Muhammad gave Clay a Muslim name: Muhammad Ali. In Arabic, "Muhammad" means "worthy of all praises" and "Ali" means "most high." Neither Malcolm X nor Muhammad Ali could have known at the time just how appropriate that name would prove to be.

At the same time, Ali's brother, Rudy, became Rahaman Ali. That name means "the one who loves."

Reporters and boxing officials reacted negatively. Many refused to use the new name. "I pity Clay and abhor what he represents," wrote noted sports reporter Jimmy Cannon.[2]

Abe Greene, commissioner of the World Boxing Association, said Clay needed to "choose between being the fighter who won the title or the fanatic leader of an extraneous force which has no place in the sports arena."[3]

The Reverend Dr. Martin Luther King, Jr., disagreed with Ali's actions as well. "When Cassius joined the Black Muslims and started calling himself Cassius X, he became a champion of racial segregation, and that is what we are fighting against," he said.[4]

Even the champion's family disapproved. "I'm not changing no name," his father said. "If he wants to do it, fine. But not me."[5]

Meanwhile, the rift between Elijah Muhammad and Malcolm X had grown worse, splintering the Nation of Islam. In the spring of 1964, Malcolm X went on a pilgrimage to the holy city of Mecca in Saudi Arabia, as all Muslims are called to do at least once. There he saw what he described as "all races, all colors—blue-eyed blonds to black-skinned Africans—in true brotherhood! In unity! Living as One! Worshiping as one! I have made sweeping indictments of all white people. I never will be guilty of that again." Statements such as these went against the separatist beliefs of Elijah Muhammad and the Nation of Islam.[6]

Soon Ali was forced to make a choice between two men he greatly admired. Malcolm X was his mentor and friend. Elijah Muhammad was the leader of the Nation of Islam. In the end, Ali chose to follow Elijah Muhammad.

On May 14, 1964, Ali left on a monthlong trip to Africa. While there, he visited Ghana, Nigeria, and Egypt. The people greeted him as a hero. He met many leaders, including Egyptian President Gamal Abdel Nasser and Ghanian President Kwame Nkrumah.

Cassius Clay, now called Muhammad Ali (center, wearing a white shirt and tie), prays with other Muslims in Egypt in 1964.

While in Ghana, his path crossed that of Malcolm X. Ali rejected his former friend, saying, "You left the honorable Elijah Muhammad. That was the wrong thing to do, Brother Malcolm." Then he turned and walked away from his former spiritual mentor.[7]

This decision haunted Ali in later years. "Turning my back on Malcolm was one of the mistakes that I regret most in my life," he later said. "I wish I'd been able to tell Malcolm I was sorry, that he was right about so many things. . . . He was a visionary—ahead of us all."[8]

Several key things happened upon Ali's return. Herbert Muhammad, a son of Elijah Muhammad, became part of his entourage. Over the years, Herbert Muhammad would come to wield a great deal of power over the champion. But the first thing he did was introduce Ali to Sonji Roi, the woman who would become his first wife.

Roi had done some modeling and was working for Herbert Muhammad in Chicago. For all his brashness regarding his boxing skills, Ali was shy around women. He immediately fell for the lively Roi. According to her, he asked her to marry him on their first date. "I wanted to be his wife and his best friend," she later said.[9]

Although he had introduced the two, Herbert Muhammad did not think Ali should marry Roi. He feared, as did others in the Nation of Islam, that she would tempt him from the strict religious path they followed. Members of the Nation of Islam did not drink. They did not smoke. They did not wear flashy clothes. Muslim women were not supposed to wear makeup or short dresses. "You don't [want to] marry this girl," Herbert Muhammad said. "She works at a cocktail place wearing one of those little bunny things on her behind."[10]

Ali, however, was smitten. He and Roi married on August 14, 1964, just over a month after they first met. Soon after, he returned to Miami to train for his upcoming rematch with Sonny Liston. The fight was set for November 16 in Boston, Massachusetts.

Almost immediately tension grew between Ali and his wife. "She wouldn't do what she was supposed to do," Ali later said. "She wore lipstick; she went into bars; she dressed in clothes that were revealing and didn't look right. She made vows, and then she broke them, and that brought on all sorts of quarreling. One time, I slapped her. It was wrong. It's the only time I did something like that, and after I slapped her I felt sorrier than she did. It hurt me more than it hurt her."[11]

Sonji Ali later recalled Ali as being a good husband. "They say religion is what kept it from working between us, that I refused to accept his religion, but that isn't true. The problem was that certain people, not Muhammad but certain other people, couldn't control me the way they wanted to. It had to do with control."[12]

Over in Liston's camp, the former champion had no such distractions. He trained hard. He believed that he had simply taken Ali too lightly the first time. This time he would have a plan. This time he would be sharp. "Fight experts who saw him during this time said that they had never seen him look so good and be so *ready*," said Pacheco.[13]

Then, just a few days before the fight, Ali suffered severe stomach pains and vomiting. He was rushed to the hospital. Doctors found that he had an inguinal hernia—a tear in the abdominal wall. Part of his intestines had broken through the tear. The situation required immediate surgery. The rematch with Liston was rescheduled for May 25, 1965.

In some ways, the delay hurt Liston more than Ali. Liston tried hard to keep his edge, but he was in his mid-thirties. At that age, a boxer's skills typically start to decline. Ali, meanwhile, was still in his early twenties. He continued to grow stronger. When he had healed from his operation, he began training again. As Pacheco put it, he was "refreshed and recharged, enjoying the considerable attention he was getting."[14]

> **"Islam is a religion and there are 750 million people all over the world who believe in it, and I'm one of them."**

Meanwhile, Malcolm X feared for his life. He believed the Nation of Islam was planning to kill him. "It's time for martyrs now," he said. "And if I'm to be one, it will be in the cause of brotherhood."[15]

On Valentine's Day, 1965, Malcolm X's house was struck by fire bombs. He and his family escaped without serious injury. He did not escape for long, however. On February 21, three gunmen murdered him as he gave a speech in New York. The killers were captured, but no one knows for sure who arranged the murder. Many suspected that Elijah Muhammad was involved.

That same night, a fire broke out in Ali's apartment. It was ruled an accident. Two days later, the Nation of Islam's headquarters building was bombed. Many believed that the bombing happened in retaliation for Malcolm X's murder. These people thought that Malcolm's followers blamed Nation of Islam leaders for his death.

"Get up and fight," he yelled.

Once again, the political turmoil affected the Ali-Liston fight. For one thing, the city of Boston no longer wished to host the bout. Instead, the small town of Lewiston, Maine, offered to take on the event. All sorts of rumors swirled around the fight. One rumor said that followers of Malcolm X would try to kill Ali before or during the fight. Another rumor said that the Nation of Islam had convinced Liston to "throw" the fight, or let Ali win.

Despite the outcome of their previous fight, most believed Liston would win the rematch. The oddsmakers made him a nine-to-five favorite. This meant that bettors who backed Liston had to bet nine dollars just to win an extra five dollars if he won. Bettors who placed just five dollars on Ali would win nine extra dollars if he won.

On the night of the fight, some three hundred police officers patrolled St. Dominic's Arena in Lewiston. They frisked the men and checked the contents of the women's handbags as they entered. They wanted to ensure that no weapons came into the arena.

A little before 10:30 P.M., the fighters entered the ring. As the challenger, Liston entered first. The small crowd booed lustily as Ali came in. It seemed ironic that Liston, who had been so hated when he was champion, should now be the fan favorite. Referee Jersey Joe Walcott, a former heavyweight champion himself, gave the fighters their prefight instructions. Ali and Liston glared at each other, as fighters often do before the bout begins.

The bell rang. Ali circled the ring clockwise, throwing left jabs and an occasional right. Liston tried to close in, but Ali moved too fast. Suddenly, less than two minutes into the fight, Ali caught Liston with a short, crisp right-hand blow to the jaw. Liston crumpled to the canvas. The punch came so fast that even many of the people attending the fight did not see it.

Turmoil followed. When a fighter knocks down his opponent, he is supposed to immediately go to a neutral corner while the referee counts. If the count reaches ten before the fallen fighter gets up, the fight is over. Ali did not go to a neutral corner. He stood over Liston as he lay on the canvas. "Get up and fight," he yelled.[16]

After several seconds, Walcott finally managed to steer Ali away. Meanwhile, Liston rolled over on the canvas, trying to get up. He got to his knees once, only to fall back down. The referee never did begin a count. Outside the ring, however, Nat Fleischer, publisher of *Ring* magazine, was keeping count.

After seventeen seconds, Liston staggered to his feet. Walcott let the fight continue. Ali attacked again as

Muhammad Ali stands over a knocked out Sonny Liston during their May 1965 bout.

Liston tried to cover up. Meanwhile, Fleischer was shouting, "It's over! He's out!" Walcott moved away from the fighters. He listened to what Fleischer was saying, then went back and stopped the fight. Ali raised his arms in victory. Less than two minutes after it had begun, the fight had ended.[17]

The controversy had just begun, however. People referred to the knockout blow as the "phantom punch."

58

Some claimed that the fight was "fixed," meaning that someone had paid to determine the outcome. Others believed that Liston had been frightened by all the talk of a possible assassination at the fight. They thought he had taken a "dive," or simply pretended to be knocked out.

After the fight, Ali watched the replay of the fight on television. Even he didn't see the knockout blow. "I'm so fast, even I missed the punch on TV," he said.[18]

Later, Ali summed it up this way: "The punch jarred him. It was a good punch, but I didn't think I hit him so hard that he couldn't have gotten up."[19]

Some time later, Liston applied for a boxing license in California. After the second Ali fight, he had claimed that he had not been badly hurt by the knockout punch. Why then, he was asked, hadn't he gotten up before the count of ten? Liston replied, "Commissioner, Muhammad Ali is a crazy man. You can't tell what a crazy man is going to do. He was standing over me, Jersey Joe couldn't control him, and if I got up, I got to put one glove on the canvas to push myself up, and as soon as my knee clears the canvas Ali is going to be beating on me. The man is crazy, and I figured I ain't getting up til someone controls him."[20]

The tape of the fight, however, reveals that Ali had moved away by the time Liston made a serious effort to get up.[21]

Boxer José Torres, who knew both fighters, believes that Liston lost both fights because Ali psyched him out. "Liston, in my estimation, quit in both fights," Torres wrote. "In the first, because initially he was completely frustrated, and then became discouraged; in the second, it was his subconscious mind. Deep down, in the innermost part of his soul, Sonny Liston feared Muhammad Ali. And, even more, he feared the Black Muslims."[22]

Still, many people saw the fight as a tainted victory for Ali. That belief, coupled with dislike and fear of the Nation of Islam, caused many people to hate Ali. But hating Ali and defeating him were two different things.

Who would be the fighter to close the mouth of the boastful Ali? The next to try was former champion Floyd Patterson. At first glance, Patterson appeared an odd choice. Liston had knocked him out twice in the first round of their two bouts. Meanwhile, Ali had defeated Liston twice.

Still, experts remained divided about Ali's true ability. On the one hand, *Sports Illustrated* writer Tex Maule said that he "may be now—and certainly can be in time—the best heavyweight ever." On the other, former heavyweight champion Joe Louis said that Ali "had a million dollars worth of confidence and a dime's worth of courage. He can't punch; he can't hurt you; and I don't think he takes a good punch. He's lucky there are no good fighters around."[23]

Ali and Patterson represented almost complete opposites. The press and public regarded the calm and polite Patterson as a gentleman. He fit the mold of what they thought a heavyweight champion should be. On the other hand, many black people were coming to see Ali as a hero. He believed in himself, and he wasn't afraid to speak out for his rights.

At first, Ali did not take Patterson seriously. After all, Patterson had twice lost badly to Liston. Ali showed up at Patterson's training camp waving a head of lettuce and some carrots. He called him "the rabbit" and said he was scared.[24]

The prefight buildup took a nasty turn when Patterson made comments about Ali's religion and refused to call him by his Muslim name. "Cassius Clay is disgracing himself and the Negro race," he said. He promised to "reclaim the title for America."[25]

Ali responded by calling Patterson a "deaf-dumb Negro who needs a good spanking." Ali promised to deliver that spanking, adding, "I want to see him cut, his ribs caved in, and then knocked out."[26]

Hating Ali and defeating him were two different things.

The bout took place November 22, 1965, in Las Vegas, Nevada. Ali kept his promise, beating and humiliating Patterson. In the first round, Ali did not bother to throw a punch. He just kept making Patterson miss. Then, in the third round, Patterson suffered a back spasm that made it difficult for him to punch or defend. Ali pounded Patterson. He knocked Patterson down in the sixth round, but Patterson rose before the count reached ten.

Several times, it appeared that Ali could have finished Patterson, but he seemed to ease off. Finally, in the twelfth round, referee Harry Krause stopped the fight. The crowd cheered the loser and booed the winner.

After the fight, the press called Ali a sadist. Joe Louis, who was critical of Ali's religion and fighting style, said: "I would have been ashamed to do it. Clay wasn't doing his best as a fighter. He was putting on a show, like wrestlers. He could have knocked out Patterson any time he really went to work, certainly no later than the sixth, when he had Floyd on the floor. Let's face it. Clay is selfish and cruel."[27]

As 1965 ended, Ali sat atop the boxing world. Still, controversy continued to swirl around him. That was nothing compared to what would come next.

Chapter 6

Living in Exile

As 1966 dawned, Muhammad Ali reigned as king of the world inside the ring, but outside he faced a whirlwind of challenges. On January 7, 1966, the courts granted him a divorce from his wife. She received an alimony settlement of fifteen thousand dollars a year for ten years plus lawyers' fees. "I am the only one to beat him," she said. "He'll remember that for the next ten years while he's making my payments."[1]

Ali agreed. For years when asked who had been his toughest opponent, he answered "my first wife."[2]

Meanwhile, Ali's life was also being affected by events taking place half a world away. By the mid-1960s, the United States had become more and more entrenched in the Vietnam War. For decades, except during World War II, France controlled Vietnam. After World War II, insurgents led by Ho Chi Minh battled against French rule. Following their defeat at the Battle of Dien Bien Phu in 1954, the French withdrew. At that point, Vietnam was partitioned into two sections. A Communist-backed regime ruled in the North, and a pro-Western government controlled the South.

Insurgents known as the Vietcong sought to overthrow the government in South Vietnam and unify the country. The Vietcong were backed by Communist powers Russia and China. The United States feared the spread of Communism throughout Asia. Therefore, the goal was to keep Communism confined to North Vietnam.

In the beginning, the United States just sent advisors to South Vietnam, but over time more and more American troops got involved. Fighting escalated, and by the end of 1965, nearly two hundred thousand American soldiers were stationed in Vietnam. To fill the need for soldiers, all American men over the age of eighteen were subject to being drafted. By July 1965, thirty-five thousand men per month were being drafted into the army.

At first, most Americans supported the war. Then, as casualties mounted, public opinion slowly began to turn. Eventually, the war polarized the nation. Many people, especially young adults who faced the chance of being drafted, opposed the war. Protests spread across college campuses and cities. Some of those who supported the war were older people who had lived through World War II and the Cold War. They believed in the government's policy to stop the spread of Communism.

Some young men evaded the draft by going to college or getting married, both of which provided an exemption for service. Others joined the National Guard or the Peace Corps. Some fled to Canada. Others applied for status as "conscientious objectors." This meant that their religious beliefs prevented them from taking part in the war.

Like other young men, Ali had registered for the draft when he turned eighteen in 1960. Just before he became heavyweight champion in 1964, he went to the Armed Forces Induction Center in Coral Gables, Florida, to take the qualifying examination. Some young men were rejected by the military as unfit for service for failing to meet physical, mental, or moral standards.

> **As a poor reader, he struggled with the mental aptitude test.**

Ali passed the physical portion of the test easily but, as a poor reader, he struggled with the mental aptitude test. He had an especially hard time doing the word problems in math. "When I looked at a lot of the questions they had on them Army tests, I just didn't know the answers," he said. "I didn't even know how to start after finding the answers."[3]

As a result, he achieved an Army IQ score of seventy-eight, which placed him in the sixteenth percentile of all those taking the test. At that time, the army did not admit anyone who scored below the thirtieth percentile. Concerned that he might not have been trying, the military retested him two months later, with three army psychologists supervising. Again he failed, and he was classified 1-Y, which meant that he was not qualified to serve.[4]

Some people thought Ali should have to serve despite his low score. In the end, Secretary of the Army Stephen Ailes wrote a letter to the chair of the House of Representatives Armed Services Committee to defend the decision not to take Ali into the army.

Ali responded to the hoopla by saying, "I only said I was the greatest, not the smartest."[5] Still, he was embarrassed at being portrayed as stupid.

The controversy over Ali's draft status cast doubt upon the future of his next boxing match.

It seemed that the matter of military service was behind him, and he could go on doing the thing he excelled at—boxing. Then, in early 1966, with the military needing more soldiers than ever, the mental aptitude percentile required for service was lowered from thirty to fifteen. Suddenly, Ali found himself eligible for the draft again.

On February 14, 1966, his lawyer requested deferment from military service for him. The request was denied, and Ali was reclassified 1-A, which meant he could be drafted at any moment. That day, he was flooded with calls from the media. Finally, when asked what he thought about the Vietcong, he answered in frustration, "Man, I ain't got no quarrel with them Vietcong."[6]

That statement became the headline for the media, and it further polarized public opinion about Ali. Many white people now viewed him as a loud-mouthed draft dodger. Many black people, however, praised his courage in standing up to the white power structure. They felt the draft was unfair. Young black men were drafted in disproportionate numbers to young white men. But Ali's antiwar stance reached beyond just the black community. Indeed, he became a symbol to the growing antiwar movement in general.

The controversy over Ali's draft status cast doubt upon the future of his next boxing match. He was scheduled to fight Ernie Terrell in Chicago, but the state's boxing commissioners ruled that the match could not take place in Illinois. They offered Ali a chance to "apologize" for his "unpatriotic comments," but he declined. "I'm not apologizing for nothing like that, because I don't have to."[7]

Promoters tried several alternate sites before finally settling on Toronto in Canada, but Terrell bowed out. Canadian heavyweight champion George Chuvalo took his place. Ali crushed Chuvalo, winning fourteen of the fifteen rounds on the judges' scorecards.

Not long before the fight, Ali applied for conscientious objector status on the grounds that going to war violated his beliefs as a Muslim. His request was denied. As part of the appeal process, he testified under oath before hearing officer Lawrence Grauman. His testimony included the following statement: "If it wasn't against my conscience to do it, I would easily do it. I wouldn't raise all this court stuff and I wouldn't go through all of this and lose the millions that I gave up and my image with the American public that I would say is completely dead and ruined because of us in here now."[8]

To the surprise of most observers, Grauman recommended that Ali's request for conscientious objector status be granted. However, the Department of Justice wrote a letter to the Appeal Board against the claim. In the end, Ali's request was denied.

That fall Ali's contract with his Louisville management expired. He chose Herbert Muhammad, son of Elijah Muhammad, to become his manager. Because Herbert Muhammad represented the Nation of Islam, this turned even more people against the champion.

Most American cities remained unwilling to host an Ali boxing match, so his next three bouts took place in Europe. Over the next few months, he stopped Henry Cooper and Brian London in matches fought in London and Karl Mildenberger in a bout held in Frankfurt. Ali dominated all of these fights.

In November, he fought Cleveland Williams in the Houston Astrodome in front of more than thirty-five thousand fans, the largest crowd ever to witness a boxing match indoors. Some experts believe this fight represented Ali at the very peak of his powers. He scored a technical knockout in just three rounds. According to some counts, he hit Williams more than a hundred times in those three rounds. In return, he absorbed just three punches. He even unveiled the footwork that became known as the "Ali Shuffle."[9]

"That night, he was the most devastating fighter who ever lived," sports commentator Howard Cosell later recalled. "He dominated from the opening bell, knocked Williams down four times, and pummeled him until

Williams was spitting blood. It was incredible that he could hand out a beating like that and not once get touched himself."[10]

On February 6, 1967, Ali returned to Houston for a bout against Ernie Terrell, a dangerous opponent who insisted on calling him Cassius Clay. Ali took his revenge in the ring by pummeling him mercilessly. He also taunted Terrell throughout the fight, demanding, "What's my name?"[11]

By the end of the fight, Terrell's face was badly swollen. Afterward, he required surgery on his damaged left eye. The vicious beating drew still more criticism for Ali. Some people believed that he held back from knocking Terrell out so he could dish out still more punishment. The bad publicity was poorly timed. People wondered how he could claim to be a conscientious objector to war and deliver such a vicious beating in the ring.

He unveiled the footwork that became known as the "Ali Shuffle."

On March 22, Ali knocked out Zora Folley in the seventh round, leading Folley to call him the greatest fighter of all time. It turned out to be Ali's last fight for three and a half years.

On April 28, Ali reported as scheduled to the induction center in Houston. When his name was called as Cassius Clay, he refused to respond. At that point, Lieutenant Clarence Hartman of the U.S. Navy took Ali to a back room and explained to him that refusing

In March 1967, Ali knocked out Zora Folley in Madison Square Garden in New York City.

to be inducted was punishable by up to five years' imprisonment and a fine. Ali responded that he knew the consequences of his refusal.

Once again, Ali entered the induction room and his name was called. Again he refused to answer. He provided a written statement stating, "I refuse to be inducted into the armed forces of the United States because I claim to be exempt as a minister of the religion of Islam."[12]

Ali added, "I strongly object to the fact that so many newspapers have given the American public and the world the impression that I have only two alternatives in taking this stand—either I go to jail or go to the Army. There is another alternative, and that is justice."[13]

Within an hour of Ali's refusal to be inducted, the New York State Athletic Commission suspended his boxing license. The commission also withdrew recognition of him as the world heavyweight champion. Other major athletic commissions soon followed suit. This made it nearly impossible for Ali to fight anywhere in the United States. Many blacks and some whites felt that this punishment was racially motivated. They believed that Ali would have been treated less harshly if he were white.

Ali's legal team filed an appeal in federal court, saying that his draft call was unconstitutional because blacks were barely represented on draft boards and blacks were being sent to Vietnam in disproportionate numbers. In fact, 31 percent of eligible black males were drafted during the war as opposed to only 18 percent of whites.

On May 8, Ali was indicted by a federal grand jury. The trial date was set for June, and he was released on five thousand dollars bail. Prosecutors suggested that if Ali accepted induction, he could enter Special Services. This would allow him to fight in exhibition matches and entertain the troops rather than participate in combat. Ali refused.

Carl Walker was an African-American lawyer who argued the prosecution's case against Ali. "The trial itself was cut and dried," he said. "Based on the law, the jury had to find him guilty."[14] Still, Walker figured that the case would eventually wind its way to the Supreme Court, which it did.

Judge Ingraham presided over the case. When the jury returned its verdict, Ingraham imposed the sentence. He sentenced Ali to five years' imprisonment and a fine of ten thousand dollars—the maximum sentence allowable. "I gave him the sentence I did because that's what he deserved," Ingraham said.[15]

Ali did not actually go to jail. His lawyers immediately filed an appeal, and he remained free. However, Judge Ingraham ordered that Ali's passport be confiscated. State commissions prevented him from fighting in the United States. Without a passport, he could not fight abroad. In effect, he was barred from fighting anywhere.

As his appeal slowly wound its way through the legal process, Ali's life went on. On August 17, 1967, he married seventeen-year-old Belinda Boyd of Chicago, Illinois. He had met her a couple of times during visits there on Nation of Islam business. Unlike his first wife, Belinda already observed the Muslim religion. She was quiet and preferred to remain in the background. "He was my first love," Belinda later recalled.[16]

In the years to come, the couple had four children: Maryum, twins Rasheeda and Jamillah, and Muhammad Junior. Ali loved his children, but he left most of the parenting to his wife. Plus, he traveled so much that he was rarely around full-time.

While Muhammad Ali was exiled from boxing, he went to colleges and universities to speak. Here, he speaks at California State College in 1968.

Unable to box, Ali soon found a new way to make money and keep his name in the public eye. He began giving lectures at college campuses. He spoke out on topics such as the war in Vietnam, being stripped of his boxing title, integration, and the notion of money versus principle. "They contained important insights that spoke to something deep inside me," he later said.[17] The government maintained surveillance on Ali during his tour, issuing a brief report after each speech.

Many people wanted to hear what Ali had to say.

At one point, a national poll revealed that he was the third-most-sought-after speaker in the country.

In December 1968, Ali actually went to jail in Dade County, Florida, not for draft evasion but for driving without a valid license. He served ten days. "Little things you take for granted like sleeping good or walking down the street, you can't do them no more," he said. "A man's got to be real serious about what he believes to say he'll do that for five years, but I was ready if I had to go."[18]

Meanwhile, Ali's case worked its way throughout the courts. On May 6, 1968, his conviction was affirmed by the Fifth Circuit Court of Appeals. Ali was disappointed. Boxing was his life, and he hated being kept away from it.

In early 1969, Ali appeared on a television program, where he said he would go back into boxing if he were allowed and if the money was right. Elijah Muhammad, thinking that this statement reflected a love for money over religion, suspended Ali from the Nation of Islam. "Mr. Muhammad Ali desired to do that which the Holy Qur'an teaches him against," Elijah Muhammad said. He also stripped Ali of his Muslim name. Ali continued to use it, however. Within a year, he was welcomed back into the fold.[19]

Ali kept busy. He participated in a filmed "computer" fight against former heavyweight champions, which featured sixteen champions in a simulated tournament. In the simulation, Ali lost to Jim Jeffries. But from this came the idea of pitting Rocky Marciano against Ali in a simulated bout. Over three days, the two men filmed seventy-five one-minute rounds. There were a variety of different endings. In the United States, Marciano knocked Ali out in the thirteenth round. In England, Ali stopped Marciano on cuts.

Soon after, Ali appeared on Broadway in a musical called *Big Time Buck White*. His performance drew praise from theater critics. "He sings with a pleasant, slightly impersonal voice, acts without embarrassment, and moves with innate dignity," wrote Clive Barnes in the *New York Times*. "He does himself proud."[20]

Meanwhile, public opinion regarding the Vietnam War was changing. More people had come to believe the war was wrong and were sympathetic to Ali and others who refused to serve. "And, unlike most war protesters, Ali had at least put his money where his mouth was, a sacrifice that did not go unnoticed even among his critics," said writer Jack Cashill.[21]

Ali began giving lectures at college campuses.

"During his exile, Muhammad Ali grew larger than sports," wrote biographer Thomas Hauser. "He became a political and social force."[22]

Still, by early 1970 Ali had grown weary of battling the government. In May he announced that he was retiring from boxing. "I don't need no prestige at beating up nobody," he said. "I'm tired. And I want to be the first black champion that got out that didn't get whipped. Fighters are just brutes that come to entertain the rich white people."[23]

Then, on June 15, 1970, the U.S. Supreme Court ruled that status as a conscientious objector could be allowed on religious grounds alone. This helped Ali's case. The government had already acknowledged that Ali was sincere in his religious beliefs. They had questioned his claim to be a pacifist. After all, according to their religion, Muslims were allowed to participate in a holy war. But, according to the Supreme Court ruling, this no longer mattered. Ali could be excused from military service based on his religious beliefs. Although Ali's specific case had not yet reached the Supreme Court, the ruling increased his chances for winning.

> "I want to be the first black champion that got out that didn't get whipped."

Ali's managers immediately wanted to put together a fight for him. Ali relented. He wanted to regain the crown he felt had been stolen from him.

Was he bitter about this part of his life, Ali was later asked? "I wasn't bitter at *all*," Ali replied. "I had a good time speaking at colleges and meeting the students . . . who supported me a hundred percent. They were as much against the Vietnam War as I was."[24]

Some people suggested that he sue the boxing commission for unjustly taking his title away. Ali declined. "Well, they only did what they thought was right and there was no need for me to try to punish them for that. It's just too bad they didn't recognize that

I was sincere in doing what *I* thought was right at the time."[25]

Some people, including former heavyweight champion Rocky Marciano, believed that Ali should not try to return to boxing. Marciano thought it would be hard to come back. It was also unclear, despite the Supreme Court ruling, whether Ali would be allowed back in the ring.

But Belinda Ali, who knew her husband best, responded. "He won it in the ring, and he'll lose it in the ring. That's the only way he'll give up his crown."[26]

Indeed, regaining his heavyweight title was more than just a goal for Muhammad Ali—it was a crusade for justice.

Chapter 7

Epic Battles

Boxing became less popular during the three and a half years without Muhammad Ali, but still it continued. The World Boxing Association held a tournament to determine Ali's successor. Ironically, Jimmy Ellis emerged as the victor. Years earlier, Ellis and Ali had fought twice as amateurs, splitting the two decisions. Ali looked forward to meeting Ellis a third time to earn back his heavyweight championship.

Joe Frazier ruined those plans. On February 16, 1970, Frazier knocked out Ellis in the fifth round. As a result, everyone recognized Frazier as world champion—everyone except Muhammad Ali.

Still, Ali held no ill will toward Frazier. "I can't blame Joe Frazier for accepting the title under the conditions he did," Ali said. "He would have fought me if he had the chance. Joe Frazier wasn't just given the title. He had to fight for it, and he had to fight the best around except for me, so I can't take nothing from him. He had to keep on living, regardless of what happened to me."[1]

Meanwhile, promoter Bob Arum tried to arrange a bout between Ali and Jerry Quarry. Ali's managers wanted him to box his way back into shape. They sought opponents they thought could push Ali—but not beat him. The slow-footed but powerful Quarry fit the bill perfectly.

Arum found it hard to find a site for the bout. Most states still refused to grant Ali a license to box. Finally, Atlanta, Georgia, offered to host the fight. The bout was scheduled for October 26, 1970.

Interest in the fight was tremendous. Many people, especially those in the black community, idolized Ali. They couldn't wait to see their hero in the ring again. Other people continued to dislike Ali. Still, even many of these people believed he had been forced out of the ring unfairly. They felt he should be allowed to fight.

Also, people were curious about how Ali would perform. He lost three and a half years from the prime of his career. Would he still be in shape? Did he still have his speed?

Ali realized just how important this fight was for his career and for his place in history. "I'm not fightin' one man," he said. "I'm fightin' a lot of men, showin' 'em here is one man they couldn't defeat, couldn't conquer, one they didn't see get big and fat and flat on his back."[2]

A host of celebrities, including notable African Americans such as comedian Bill Cosby, actor Sidney

Poitier, and civil rights leaders Jesse Jackson and Coretta Scott King, turned out to see Ali's return. And a grand return it was. In the third round, Ali opened a huge cut over Quarry's eye. The referee stopped the fight.

Just six weeks later, on December 7, Ali fought Oscar Bonavena in New York. The first fourteen rounds were fairly dull. But in the final round, Ali knocked Bonavena down three times and won the fight.

After this fight, the boxing world demanded a bout between Ali and Frazier. It was one of the most anticipated fights in boxing history. Both were former Olympic champions. Ali was undefeated as a professional. Frazier had won twenty-six fights in a row—twenty-three of them by knockout.

The two men also had totally opposite styles. That made the matchup even more intriguing. Ali liked to dance around his opponent and score with his long jab. Frazier, meanwhile, constantly pushed forward. He stalked his opponent until he saw an opening. Then he pounced, often with a devastating left hook. He did not mind taking three or four punches to set up one or two of his own.

Boxer Henry Cooper said this about Frazier: "You could hit Frazier with your Sunday punch and you could break your hand. He'd shake his head and come on after you."[3]

As the bout drew close, excitement peaked. Everywhere, people, not just boxing fans, talked about "The Fight." Each fighter received $2.5 million, a record purse.

This bout marked the first in a series of epic battles

that Ali would fight against Frazier, Ken Norton, and George Foreman. These fights would cement his status as a boxing legend but take a tremendous toll on his body.

The Ali-Frazier fight divided fans. Most African Americans backed Ali, even though both fighters were black. Frazier was viewed as solid and dull. Ali was flamboyant and exciting. Furthermore, black America respected Ali for standing up to the white establishment by refusing to be drafted. Meanwhile, many white fans backed Frazier. They found him much more appealing than the brash Ali.

Boxing became less popular during the three and a half years without Muhammad Ali, but still it continued.

Ali fueled the fire by portraying himself as the champion of black people and Frazier as a tool of the white establishment. He said things like, "Any black person who's for Joe Frazier is a traitor."[4]

Ali even bought a house in Philadelphia so he could train near Frazier (and get under his skin). Ali said he was smarter than Frazier. He said he was better looking than Frazier. Indeed, Ali claimed that he was the "prettiest" of any fighter because he was hit so rarely with strong punches from his opponents.

To Ali, this was all part of the act to stir up interest in the fight. Frazier, however, took the insults personally. He vowed to shut Ali's mouth by beating him in the ring.

The fight took place on March 8, 1971, at Madison

Square Garden in New York City. It was one of those rare sporting events that truly lived up to its hype. The fight seesawed back and forth. Ali won the early rounds, scoring with his jab as Frazier tried to move in close. But Frazier kept up the pressure. In the middle rounds, he began to drive Ali into the ropes, where he battered Ali's body with heavy blows. This started to slow down Ali.

Still, by the end of the tenth round, Frazier's face was puffed up and his eyes were closing. Yet he continued moving forward. In the eleventh round he rocked Ali with a left hook, but Ali managed to survive the round. At the end of round fourteen, most people thought the fight was very even. It seemed that the final three minutes would decide the fight.

"Expectation is still the word to use to describe the excited crowd," recalled José Torres. "No one is sure who is ahead. Some say Ali, some say Frazier, but nobody is yelling one-sided."[5]

In the decisive fifteenth round, Frazier hit Ali with a thunderous left hook that sent him to the canvas. Despite being dead tired, Ali quickly climbed to his feet, and the fight continued. Frazier won the decision in what came to be known as "The Fight of the Century." The battle left both fighters bloodied and bruised. Both had to go to the hospital once the fight ended.

After the fight, the media wanted to interview Ali. At first, Angelo Dundee tried to prevent this. But Ali intervened. He proved to be as gracious in defeat as he was boastful in victory. "They know I always talk after a victory," he said. "Now I've got to talk after a loss.

Sports Illustrated

MARCH 15 1971   60 CENTS

END OF THE ALI LEGEND

This 1971 *Sports Illustrated* cover shows Joe Frazier throwing a punch at Muhammad Ali.

Let them hear how I lost. Let the people who believe in me see that I'm not crushed, that I've had a defeat just as they have defeats, that I'll get up and come back again, just like other people do."[6]

Ali said he hoped people would remember the art and the science of his boxing. But, as Ferdie Pacheco noted, "what we remembered was his courage, his toughness, and his championship heart."[7] Meanwhile, Ali was already planning for a rematch.

> "Let the people who believe in me see that I'm not crushed. . ."

Then, on June 28, 1971, exactly four years after Ali had refused to be inducted into the Army, the U.S. Supreme Court unanimously voted to reverse his conviction. The Court noted that there are three basic tests for conscientious objector status that the Justice Department in its case on behalf of the U.S. government had claimed Ali did not meet:

> An applicant's objection must be against all war. (The Justice Department pointed out that Ali did not object to holy war as decreed by Allah.)

> The applicant's objection must be based on religious training and belief. (The Justice Department claimed that the teachings of the Nation of Islam were primarily political rather than religious.)

> The applicant's objection must be sincere. (The Justice Department questioned Ali's sincerity.)[8]

Before the Supreme Court, the government conceded the latter two points. Still, they said Ali was not entitled to conscientious objector status based on the first test. But the Court ruled that "since the Appeal Board gave no reasons for its denial of the petitioner's claim, there is absolutely no way of knowing upon which of the three grounds offered in the Department's letter it relied. Yet the Government now acknowledges that two of those grounds were not valid. And the Government's concession aside, it is indisputably clear, for the reasons stated, that the Department was simply wrong as a matter of law in advising that the petitioner's beliefs were not religiously based and were not sincerely held."[9]

Therefore the Supreme Court ruled 8-0 (with Justice Thurgood Marshall abstaining) in favor of Muhammad Ali. At that point, all charges against him were dropped. By ruling very narrowly on the specifics of Ali's particular case, the Court prevented other members of the Nation of Islam from thinking that they, too, could all receive conscientious objector status.

With his legal troubles behind him, Ali set out in earnest to regain his heavyweight title. His next fight came on July 26, 1971, against his boyhood friend and former sparring partner, Jimmy Ellis. He knocked out Ellis in the twelfth round. Later that year he won a lopsided decision over Buster Mathis and a knockout victory over Jurgen Blin of West Germany.

In 1972, Ali fought often, defeating Mac Foster, George Chuvalo, Jerry Quarry in a rematch, and Al Lewis. In addition, he was offered the lead role in a movie called *Heaven Can Wait*. The script had been written by Francis Ford Coppola, who later went on to direct *The Godfather* and many other famous movies. Ali thought the offer sounded interesting. However, the movie involved an athlete's reincarnation. Based on that, Elijah Muhammad would not approve the project. He thought the script ran counter to the Muslim religion.[10]

In 1972, Ali fulfilled a longtime dream by opening a training camp at Deer Lake, Pennsylvania. The six-acre camp reminded him of Archie Moore's Salt Mine camp, where he had trained early in his career. He built a gymnasium and cabins for his family and friends. One cabin was even used as a mosque. He trained at Deer Lake for victories against Floyd Patterson and Bob Foster late in 1972.

Ali next hoped to schedule a rematch with Frazier. Those plans were derailed in January 1973 when George Foreman knocked Frazier out to win the championship. In February, Ali won a lackluster decision over Joe Bugner. Ali appeared for that bout attired in a robe inscribed "People's Choice"—a gift from singing legend Elvis Presley.

In March, Ali fought against a lightly regarded young heavyweight named Ken Norton. In the second round Norton caught Ali with a strong right. In Ali's corner at the end of the round, Dundee and Pacheco realized that their fighter's jaw was fractured. In the brief time between rounds, they tried to decide what to do. As a doctor, Pacheco knew that the fight should be stopped. But he also knew that a loss to the unheralded Norton might cripple Ali's chances of fighting for the title

In 1973, rock and roll legend Elvis Presley gave Muhammad Ali this colorful robe. The robe is now on display at the Muhammad Ali Center in Kentucky.

again. "Even after being told his jaw was broken, Ali emphatically refused to have the fight stopped," Pacheco recalled. "In his champion's heart, Ali felt he could beat Norton."[11]

The fight went twelve grueling rounds. Going into the final round, the bout was nearly even. Norton won the final round and the decision. Immediately after the fight, Ali had an operation to repair his broken jaw. The hardest part was that he had trouble talking for some time.

Those who disliked Ali delighted in seeing him defeated by a lesser fighter. Even some of his supporters thought the loss might mark the end of Ali's career. "Losing to Norton was the end of the road, at least as far as I could see," said sportscaster Howard Cosell.[12]

Ali thought otherwise. And, oddly enough, his courage in continuing to fight despite his fractured jaw raised his esteem among many people. "In losing to Norton, he actually won," Pacheco said. "He won the respect of his boxing peers. They knew from the Frazier fight that he was tough, from the Norton fight, they learned *how* tough."[13]

They also saw Ali's gracious side. He refused to blame his defeat on his broken jaw. "Norton beat me today," Ali said. "Fair and square. I tried to win, but he was too tough today. Tomorrow, when I get well, I'll go out and whup [him], but today, Norton was the better man."[14]

It took Ali more than a day to get well. Indeed, it took six months before a rematch could be scheduled.

This time Ali won a unanimous decision. His latest comeback was underway. He followed up just six weeks later with a win against Rudi Lubbers in a bout fought in Indonesia.

Then came Ali's chance to avenge his loss to Frazier. In the weeks leading up to the fight, Ali taunted Frazier, calling him "ignorant," which infuriated Frazier. The two nearly came to blows at an event with Howard Cosell a few days before the actual fight. They were watching film of the first fight and commenting on it. Eventually, insults started flying. Frazier wrestled Ali to the floor. The two had to be separated.

Most viewers thought that Ali was playing around, as he often did. Cosell, however, realized that Frazier was not kidding. Cosell was genuinely scared, fearing that someone would get hurt. Ali, too, became alarmed when he realized

He refused to blame his defeat on his broken jaw.

Frazier was serious. Both fighters were fined five thousand dollars.[15]

The actual fight was almost anticlimactic. This time Ali managed to dictate the pace of the fight. He won a unanimous decision. Frazier immediately demanded another rematch.

In the meantime, Ali was on his way to one of the most spectacular fights of his entire career—a bout with George Foreman that took place in the African nation of Zaire. This bout became known as "The Rumble in the Jungle."

Like Sonny Liston a decade earlier, many people considered Foreman unbeatable. He had won forty fights with no losses. All but three of the fights had ended in knockouts. "Sooner or later," wrote Dave Anderson of the *New York Times,* "the champion will land one of his sledgehammer punches, and for the first time in his career, Muhammad Ali will be counted out."[16]

Both fighters arrived early in Zaire to train. Ali, as always, drew crowds wherever he went. He continued to entertain people with his wit and his poetry. In one poem, he promised that he would once again "float like a butterfly, sting like a bee," adding that Foreman's "hands can't hit what his eyes can't see."[17]

Just eight days before the fight, Foreman sustained a cut over his right eye. The fight had to be postponed for

In September 1974, Muhammad Ali was set to fight George Foreman in Zaire. People cheered when Ali drove past them.

a month while Foreman healed. Both fighters were tired of Zaire. They wanted to get the fight over so they could go home.

The fight took place at 4 A.M. on October 30, 1974. The time difference allowed it to be seen in the evening in the United States. Sixty thousand screaming fans filled the stadium. "Ali, bomaye," they chanted, meaning, "Ali, kill him."[18] Still, few experts believed Ali could stay with Foreman.

Ali realized he could no longer dance around the ring for the entire fight to avoid Foreman's powerful punches. Therefore, he unveiled a new strategy that baffled the audience, but that proved effective in the end. "What Ali did in the ring that night was truly inspired," said Ferdie Pacheco. "The layoff had taken away his first set of gifts, so in Zaire he developed another. . . . Ali figured out that the way to beat George Foreman was to let Foreman hit him."[19]

Basically, Ali's strategy consisted of leaning back against the ropes. Round after round he let Foreman pound him with heavy blows as he covered up. Sometimes he would launch a counterattack and pepper Foreman with jabs. Still, it seemed certain Ali could not continue to absorb so many punches. Surely he must fall.

But Ali knew that Foreman had rarely fought more than a few rounds at a time. Usually he knocked out his opponents early in the bout. After the seventh round, Ali sensed that Foreman was running out of gas. But Ali was growing tired, too. He decided to try for a knockout. In the eighth round, the two fighters stood toe to toe. They traded heavy blows.

Then Ali caught Foreman with a strong right. The champion toppled to the canvas. Foreman struggled to his feet, but the count had reached ten. The fight was over. Ali's strategy, which he dubbed "rope a dope," had worked.

"I take nothing away from George," Ali said after the bout. "He can still beat any man in the world. Except me."[20]

In one poem, Ali promised that he would once again "float like a butterfly, sting like a bee."

Foreman had trouble accepting defeat. At first he claimed that someone had slipped something into his water that made him groggy. Years later, however, he admitted, "He beat me fair and square. The guy could fight. He could punch."[21]

Once again, Ali reigned as champion of the world. *Sports Illustrated* named him Sportsman of the Year. President Gerald Ford invited him to White House. He seemed more popular than ever.

In early 1975, Elijah Muhammad died. Ali missed his spiritual leader, but he continued training for his next battle. In March 1975, Ali easily defended his crown against Chuck Wepner, knocking out the challenger in the final round. But Wepner did knock Ali down in the ninth round. Ali said that Wepner was standing on his foot when he threw the punch, causing him to slip. Referee Tony Perez ruled it a knockdown, though.

That knockdown of a world-famous champion by a less-skilled fighter, a "journeyman," inspired a struggling actor named Sylvester Stallone. From that moment came the idea for the blockbuster series of *Rocky* movies. "Everybody wants a slice of immortality, whether it's for fifteen rounds in a fight or two minutes in their own life," Stallone said. "They want that sensation that they have a shot at the impossible dream, and that solidified the whole thing for me."[22]

Ali kept busy, defeating Ron Lyle by knockout in May. Less than two months later, he defeated Joe Bugner in a rematch held in Kuala Lumpur, Malaysia. That fight was just a prelude to the third Ali-Frazier bout, which remains one of the greatest fights of all time. Held in the Philippines, the Ali-Frazier fight was dubbed "The Thrilla in Manila."

Ali faced a number of distractions leading up to the fight. He didn't bring his wife to the Philippines. Instead, he brought a woman named Veronica Porsche. Tall and beautiful, Porsche had entered a beauty contest in 1974 to serve as a poster girl for the Ali-Foreman fight. She was one of four women chosen to travel throughout the United States promoting the fight. She also went to Zaire. Ali was smitten with her beauty, and the two began an affair.

Ali took Porsche to a party at the presidential palace in Manila, where it was assumed that she was his wife. The news soon got back to his wife, Belinda. She immediately flew to Manila. There she confronted her husband. Just one day later, she flew home.

"I used to chase women all the time," Ali later recalled. "And I won't say it was right, but look at all the temptations I had. . . . Women were always offering themselves to me."[23]

Even as Ali's marriage crumbled, he continued to prepare for the big fight. He also played with Frazier's mind. As the fight neared, Ali taunted Frazier. One day at a meeting with the press, Ali pulled out a black rubber gorilla out of his pocket and pounded it. On and on went the taunting. Through it all, Frazier got madder and madder. He said nothing. He vowed to let his fists do the talking.

The fight was a classic—one of the best ever. It was fought at 10:45 A.M. on October 1, 1975. That way it could be shown on closed-circuit television in the evening in the United States.

The fight seesawed back and forth. Ali won the early rounds, staggering Frazier several times. In the middle rounds, Frazier rocked Ali. But in the later rounds, Ali pummeled Frazier's face. Frazier's eyes swelled almost shut. By the end of the fourteenth round, he could barely see. Still, he wanted to continue. His trainer, Eddie Futch, refused to let him come out for the final round. "Sit down, son, it's over," Futch said. "But no one will ever forget what you did here today."[24]

Over in his corner, Ali could barely stand. He wasn't sure he could fight another round. He didn't have to. He had won.

After the fight, both fighters looked terrible. Ali attended a reception given by Ferdinand Marcos, the

In 1975, Ali fought Joe Frazier in Manila, Philippines. Ali won in fourteen rounds.

leader of the Philippines. He could barely eat or talk. "It was like death," Ali said. "Closest thing to dyin' that I know of."[25]

A few miles away, Frazier was in bed, trying to recover. "Man, I hit him with punches that'd bring down the walls of a city," he said. "Lawdy, Lawdy, he's a great champion."[26]

Years later, Ali would still cite that fight as a highlight of his career. Frazier "brought out the best in me, and the best fight we fought was in Manila," he said.[27]

Ali had regained his championship. He had won some of the most classic fights in history. He was arguably the most famous person in the entire world. What would he do next?

After his bruising battle in Manila, Ali chose an easier opponent. He knocked out Belgian champion Jean-Pierre Coopman is just five rounds. Next Ali battled Jimmy Young in what was supposed to be an easy bout. But Ali came in slow and overweight, and won a lackluster decision. Less than a month later, on May 24, 1976, he knocked out England's Richard Dunn in the fifth round.

These epic bouts had all taken a toll on Ali's body.

Ali's next appearance proved to be one of the most embarrassing of his career. He fought in Japan against Japanese professional wrestler Antonio Inoki. The bout was billed as boxing versus wrestling. Inoki crab-walked around the ring for fifteen rounds to keep Ali from hitting him. Meanwhile, he aimed kicks at Ali's legs. Ali got in a few jabs, but only a few. The dull contest was declared a draw. In disgust, spectators showered the ring with seat cushions and drink cans. Even worse, Inoki's kicks caused blood clots in Ali's legs. He had to go to the hospital when he got back to the United States.

Next, Ali faced a much tougher opponent, fighting Ken Norton for a third time. Like their first two battles, this one seesawed back and forth. Norton won the early rounds. Then Ali stormed back. Going into the final round the bout was nearly even. But Ali finished strong to win the decision.

Still, it was evident that Ali's skills were declining. He could no longer dance away from opponents' punches. He survived with strength, courage, and his ability to take heavy punches and battle back. But these epic bouts had all taken a toll on Ali's body.

Boxing is a young man's game, and the champion was growing older. Many people, even some of his friends and advisors, began to question whether he should retire while he was still on top of the world.

Chapter 8

Falling Star

You see it time and time again—superstars in any profession who press on too long after their prime.

It happens with top boxers as well. They think they have one more good fight left in them. They see one more big payday. Then they'll retire. Just one more fight. And then just one more after that. And one more after that.

It happened to Muhammad Ali. He could have retired a hero after defeating George Foreman in Zaire. He could have retired a hero after beating Joe Frazier in "The Thrilla in Manila." He could have retired a hero after defeating Ken Norton in their third fight.

But, like so many others, Ali fell prey to the "one more fight" syndrome. He waited more than seven months before climbing into the ring for his next bout. There he won a boring victory against the overmatched Alfredo Evangelista of Spain.

Meanwhile, Ali was dealing with struggles outside

the ring. In September 1976, Belinda Ali filed for divorce. Ali's affair with Veronica Porsche continued. Belinda Ali saw no way to keep the marriage going. She received a generous divorce settlement, and Muhammad Ali also placed one million dollars in a trust fund for their four children. "The whole time we were married, I tried to accept what he was about and what he liked," she later said. "And then everything got destroyed."[1]

On June 19, 1977, Ali married Veronica Porsche. They had lived together for some time and already had a ten-month-old child, Hana. They went to Hawaii on their honeymoon. Ali seemed bored. He spent much of his time signing autographs.

The public remained hungry for material about Ali. In 1975, he published his autobiography, *The Greatest: My Own Story,* coauthored with Richard Durham. Herbert Muhammad had demanded approval of the manuscript. As a result, many people felt that the book was not nearly as candid as it might have been.

The book was followed in 1977 by a movie titled *The Greatest,* which starred Ali. Actor Ernest Borgnine played Angelo Dundee. Some members of Ali's entourage also appeared in the movie. In general, the movie drew praise from viewers and critics alike. *New York Times* film reviewer Vincent Canby said that the film "never distorts or disguises the extraordinary presence and complex personality of the man who began his career as Cassius Clay."[2]

The film also featured the beautiful soundtrack song "The Greatest Love of All," recorded by George Benson.

In 1977, Ali starred in a movie called *The Greatest*.

Later, Whitney Houston recorded a version of the song that became a huge hit.

On September 29, 1977, Ali stepped into the ring again for a bout against Earnie Shavers. Shavers was a dangerous foe. He had won more than fifty fights. He also possessed one of the hardest punches in all of boxing. A sellout crowd packed Madison Square Garden. Another 70 million people watched the fight live on television.

Despite absorbing some hard blows, including a right hand in the second round that rocked him, Ali was well ahead through most of the fight. Shavers came on strong toward the end. Some wondered if Ali would survive the final round. But Ali, with his champion's heart, drew deep on his reserves and fought a masterful fifteenth round to secure the decision.

"Fighting Ali was probably the greatest thing in my whole fight career," Shavers said. "When Ali fought, the whole world stopped and watched for an hour, and the fact that I did well opened up a lot of doors for me."[3]

Teddy Brenner of Madison Square Garden thought Ali should retire after the Shavers fight. "The trick in boxing is to get out at the right time, and the fifteenth round last night was the right time for Ali," Brenner said. He backed that up by vowing that he would never again let Ali fight in Madison Square Garden.[4]

After fights, boxers are required to give a urine specimen. This allows doctors to ensure that they haven't been taking performance-enhancing drugs. Ali's specimen following the Shavers fight showed no signs of drugs, but it did reveal something even more alarming. Not only was there blood in the urine, but entire sections of cells from tubules.

As Ferdie Pacheco, Ali's long-time fight doctor explained, "These cells filter the blood and make urine. They are not replaceable. They scar and impair kidney function." In short, their presence in his urine could indicate potentially serious kidney damage.[5]

Pacheco hoped to convince Ali to retire. He wrote a letter explaining the lab results and recommending that Ali not fight again. He sent copies to Ali, his wife, and three of his closest advisors. He did not receive a single response.

At that point, Pacheco left his role as Ali's doctor. "When Ali wouldn't quit the exciting world of boxing, I did," Pacheco wrote. "If a national treasure like Ali could not be saved, at least I didn't have to be a part of his undoing."[6]

Ali wanted to keep fighting. His managers and entourage wanted him to keep fighting, too. They wanted him to keep bringing in the money. His managers promised to find him "easy" fights. Soon they came up with an easy opponent who Ali really wanted to fight—Leon Spinks. Spinks had won an Olympic gold medal at the 1976 Olympics. Ali had beaten three Olympic gold-medal winners: Floyd Patterson, Joe Frazier, and George Foreman. He wanted to beat a fourth. Also, the inexperienced Spinks, who had only a handful of professional fights, seemed like an easy target.

Even smooth-talking Ali did not know how to hype the fight. "What am I gonna tell people, that I'm gonna destroy him?" he said. "Talking that way makes me look stupid, so I ain't gonna talk."[7]

Ali didn't take the fight as seriously as he should have. He weighed 242 pounds when he began training, far above his ideal fighting weight. Furthermore, he didn't train hard. He sparred only twenty rounds before the bout.[8]

The fight itself, held on February 15, 1978, in Las Vegas, was dull. Ali spent much of the fight on the ropes, letting the awkward Spinks pummel his arms and body. Ali hoped Spinks would tire, but the young man just kept punching. Ali tried to rally in the last round, but it was too little, too late. Spinks won a split decision.

Ali wanted to keep fighting.

"Of all the fights I lost in boxing, losing to Spinks hurt the most," Ali said. "That's because it was my own fault. Leon fought clean; he did the best he could. But it was embarrassing that someone with so little fighting skills could beat me. I didn't train right."[9]

Ali wanted a rematch. He wanted a chance to atone for his poor performance. The fight was scheduled for September 1978. This time Ali trained hard. He wanted the chance to become the first three-time champion of the world.

"Never have I suffered like I'm forcing myself to suffer now," Ali told Pat Putnam of *Sports Illustrated*.

"I've worked this hard for a fight before, but never, never for this long. . . . All the time, I'm in pain; I hurt all over. I hate it, but I'm taking it. I know this is my last fight, and it's the last time I'll ever have to do it. I don't want to lose and then spend the rest of my life looking back and saying, '. . . I should have trained harder.'"[10]

The rematch took place on September 15, 1978, in New Orleans. The fight itself was lackluster, but the drama grew with each round. Millions of viewers around the world wondered if Ali could become champion for the third time. No fighter had ever done that. The crowd roared when Ali prevailed by unanimous decision. It was a fitting way to close what seemed to be the final chapter of Ali's remarkable boxing career.

> "I know this is my last fight, and it's the last time I'll ever have to do it."

Even Ali acknowledged that it was time to quit. "I'd be the biggest fool in the world to go out a loser after being the first three-time champ," he told one reporter.[11] On June 26, 1979, he announced his retirement from boxing.

In the meantime, he starred in a television miniseries called *Freedom Road*. Ali played the role of an ex-slave who fought in the Civil War and later became a U.S. senator. His costar, Kris Kristofferson, thought Ali had promise as an actor. "I thought he was an honest performer," Kristofferson said. "In my view, he could have had a career as an actor, but nobody took the time to train him properly."[12]

Soon after, Ali and Veronica moved to a mansion in Los Angeles. By this time, they had a second daughter, Laila, who was one year old. Ali's four children from his marriage to Belinda lived in Chicago with their grandparents. Ali had also fathered two other children outside of marriage while still married to Belinda.

Although the mansion seemed lavish, the quiet life bored Ali. Floyd Patterson visited him and thought he seemed lonely. "He goes out in the morning in his Rolls Royce with the top down, looking for people to recognize him," Patterson said.[13]

In truth, Ali missed boxing. Part of the lure was money. Over the years, Ali had earned more in the ring than all the previous heavyweight champions combined. He had made millions more from various business ventures and endorsements. But much of Ali's money was already gone. Friends and acquaintances all agreed that he was incredibly generous with his money. He also made some bad business investments. Some say that members of his entourage also took advantage of him.

In early 1980, President Jimmy Carter asked Ali to travel on a diplomatic trip to Africa. The president wanted Ali to convince African countries to join the United States in boycotting the 1980 Olympics in Moscow. This was in response to the Russian invasion of Afghanistan in December 1979. The trip was a disaster. It damaged Ali's reputation. Most Africans did not support the idea of a boycott. Some felt offended at the pressure from the United States.

Tanzanian President Julius Nyerere refused to even

see Ali. At that point, Ali said, "If I'm to be looked at as an Uncle Tom or a traitor or someone against my black brothers, I want out, 'cause that's not my purpose."[14]

After this negative publicity, Ali felt drawn back to boxing, where he truly felt comfortable. He missed the spotlight, too. In addition, he knew he could make millions by climbing back into the ring. In March 1980, he agreed to fight again.

Not everyone supported his decision. His mother, Odessa Clay, told a reporter, "I just don't want him to fight anymore."[15]

In the end, Ali signed to fight reigning heavyweight champion Larry Holmes, who had been one of Ali's sparring partners in the 1970s. Ali was to receive $8 million for the fight. Holmes, even as champion, received much less. Holmes did not want to fight Ali. He respected and loved the former champion. He was afraid he might hurt Ali.

Others were concerned about Ali's health as well. They noticed that he was speaking more slowly and softly. Prior to the fight, Ali underwent a two-day evaluation at the famed Mayo Clinic in Minnesota. He needed to do this in order to get his license from the Nevada State Athletic Commission for the fight, which would take place in Las Vegas.

"In summary," concluded a report from the Mayo Clinic, "there is no specific finding that would prohibit him from engaging in further prize fights. There is minimal evidence of some difficulty with his speech and memory and perhaps to a very slight degree with his coordination. All of these are more noticeable when he is fatigued."[16]

This report would not be alarming to a normal person, but it raised warning signals about a man who was preparing for a heavyweight title fight. Still, the bout remained on schedule.

Ali trained hard for the fight, but he was thirty-eight years old. He had lost much of his speed and his stamina.

However, he looked great when he entered the ring that night. He came in at 217 pounds. People said he looked like the "old Ali." Some thought he could recapture the magic of years past. Holmes knew better: he crushed Ali that night. The fight was stopped after ten rounds. Holmes had won every round. Many people thought Holmes held back from trying to knock out Ali.

Others were concerned about Ali's health as well.

"He tricked everyone," Holmes said later. "He looked good. But sometimes the mind makes a date the body can't keep."[17]

"Before the fight started, I thought I could win," Ali said after the fight. "But after the first round, I knew I was in trouble. I was tired, nothing left at all."[18]

For his part, Holmes felt awful after the fight. He recalled that he went to Ali's room and told him, "You're still the greatest . . . I want people to know I'm proud I learned my craft from Ali. I'm prouder of sparring with him when he was young than I am of beating him when he was old."[19]

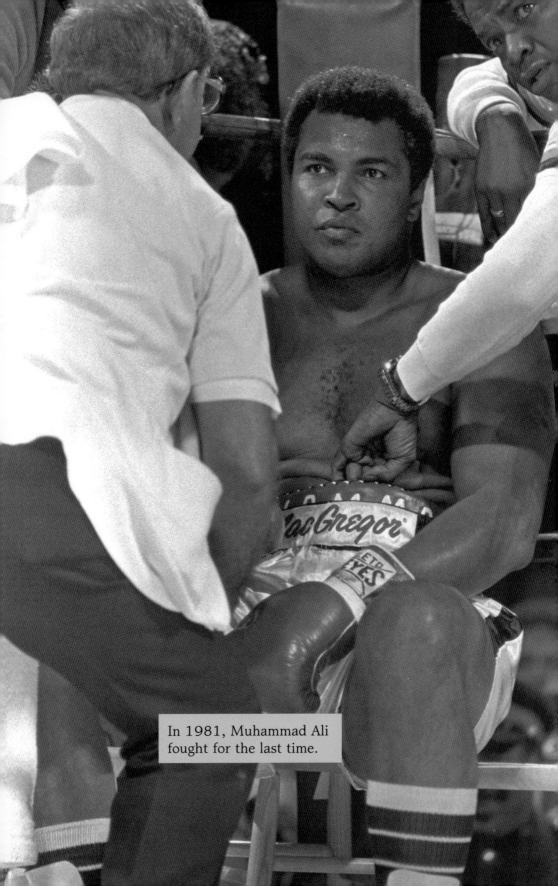

In 1981, Muhammad Ali fought for the last time.

The Holmes fight further damaged Ali's credibility as a fighter. The situation worsened when it was revealed that Ali had been taking thyroid medication prior to the bout. Many felt he shouldn't have fought while taking the drug.

Then, in 1981, Ali's name was dragged into a $21-million scandal. A man named Harold Smith had formed two organizations called Muhammad Ali Amateur Sports (MAAS) and Muhammad Ali Professional Sports (MAPS) to promote boxing events. Ali lent his name to the groups in return for a share of the net profits. The organizations lost lots of money, which was covered by Wells Fargo Bank of California. Smith went to prison for embezzlement. Although Ali had no involvement in the wrongdoing, his reputation suffered.

Meanwhile, Ali planned to fight yet again. He couldn't bear the thought of ending his career on such a low note as the Holmes fight. He thought the thyroid medicine he was taking at the time was the reason he had performed so poorly. He wanted to make amends. A bout was set with Trevor Berbick for December 11, 1981, in the Bahamas.

Ali's family and many of his close friends wanted him to quit fighting. His daughter Maryum, who was twelve at the time, said, "I pretty much accepted my father fighting up until he fought Trevor Berbick. That was the only fight I wanted him to lose. I wanted him to win but I didn't, because if he won he'd keep fighting, and I didn't want him to fight anymore."[20]

Berbick won a unanimous decision in a lackluster battle. After the fight, Ali acknowledged that his boxing career was over for good. "I think I'm too old. I was slow. I was weak. Nothing but Father Time," he said. "I lost, but I lost honorably."[21]

Now it was time for Muhammad Ali to move on with the rest of his life. But he was destined to battle a foe more dangerous than any he had faced in the ring.

Chapter 9

The Legend Lives On

Ali lived for boxing, and he missed it. Without it he seemed somewhat lost and lonely. Friends also worried about his health. Even toward the end of his boxing career, his speech sometimes seemed slow and slurred. To many of his friends, the symptoms now seemed to be growing worse.

After visiting Ali at his mansion, Alex Haley, the author of *Roots,* observed that "even though he had the big mansion and the gorgeous wife, he seemed very much alone. He was kind of just floating around. The entourage wasn't there anymore; he knew he'd never fight again. He looked lonely, and I felt sorry for him."[1]

Ali tried to keep busy. He still traveled often. He spent more time with his children. He has acknowledged feeling bad that his career often prevented him from being home for milestones such as his children's first words and first days at school. "Some of my children saw me more on television than in person, and spoke to me most often over the phone," he said. "I sincerely regret that loss to them and to me."[2]

But more time at home also created new stresses. Ali and Veronica began to argue. She had hoped to pursue her own career once he stopped boxing. Ali, however, adhered to the traditional view of women. He wanted her to remain at home. He wanted her to wear long clothes and keep her head covered. "I did adhere to a lot of his wishes," Veronica later said, "but it was pretty much an old-fashioned way of living."[3]

After eight days, doctors concluded that Ali had mild symptoms of Parkinson's syndrome.

Meanwhile, Ali grew more and more worried about his health. He often felt tired. Sometimes his speech was slurred. He told his doctor that he was "walking like an old man."[4]

In July 1982, Ali checked into the UCLA Medical Center. After a series of tests, doctors found no serious problems. Still he felt tired much of the time. On a trip back to Louisville, he had lunch with his old friend Yolanda "Lonnie" Williams. He had known Lonnie since 1962, when he was twenty and she was just five. Their families were neighbors in Louisville. She recalled that he was like a big brother to her when she was little. He had taken her to the playground and recited poetry to her.

In the years since, Lonnie had gone to college. She had a good job as an account representative for Kraft Foods. She also was working on an MBA degree at the University of Louisville. She grew alarmed when she saw Ali. He stumbled and seemed depressed. After their lunch together, she made a life-changing decision. She decided to give up her career and move to Los Angeles. She got a condominium near Ali's mansion and began caring for him. "Muhammad took care of all my expenses," she said, "with Veronica's knowledge and consent. And I did everything I could for him."[5]

Still, Ali's health continued to decline. In September 1984, he checked into the Columbia-Presbyterian Medical Center in New York for a series of tests. "I'm not suffering," he told reporters, "I'm in no pain." Still, he was always tired, and his speech was slurred. "I'm not scared, but my family and friends are scared to death."[6]

After eight days, doctors concluded that Ali had mild symptoms of Parkinson's syndrome. Doctors also said that Ali did not suffer from dementia pugilistica, commonly referred to as "punch-drunkenness."

"He's got a problem with his brain in terms of motor control," said neurologist Stanley Fahn of Columbia-Presbyterian. "We expect he'll respond to medication. After the medication, he should live as normal a life as possible."[7]

Doctors pointed out that there is a difference between Parkinson's syndrome and Parkinson's disease. The disease is a brain disorder caused when nerve cells in a certain part of the brain die or become impaired. When functioning normally, these cells produce a vital chemical called dopamine. Dopamine allows the body's muscles and movement to function in a coordinated manner. When approximately 80 percent of the dopamine-producing cells are damaged, the symptoms of Parkinson's disease appear. These symptoms include shaking, slowness of movement, stiffness, and difficulty with balance. Other symptoms may include facial stiffness, a shuffling walk, and muffled speech. The disease typically worsens over time.

Other people may show similar symptoms but not have Parkinson's disease. These people are said to have parkinsonism or Parkinson's syndrome. The symptoms may or may not get worse. In Ali's case, doctors at first thought that medication might relieve some of his symptoms.

Not everyone agreed with the diagnosis. Ali's longtime fight doctor, Ferdie Pacheco, maintained that at least some of Ali's problems were caused by blows absorbed in the ring. Over the years, Pacheco had followed the careers of dozens of boxers. He saw many of them exhibit symptoms of brain damage as a result of fighting. He saw many of the same symptoms in Ali. "Muhammad Ali progressed with shocking rapidity from boxing-induced neurological damage to a Parkinson-like symptomatology," Pacheco said.[8]

Indeed, over time his doctors came to the same conclusion. Years later, Dr. Stanley Fahn said that Ali had requested during his initial treatment that Fahn not state publicly what he thought caused his problems. But for Thomas Hauser's biography, Ali asked Fahn to speak freely. Fahn then said that he believed Ali's problem "was a post-traumatic Parkinsonism due to injuries from fighting. Muhammad himself told me he thinks that most of the damage came from the third Frazier fight, the one in Manila. That may be where he started to get his damage, but it's highly unlikely that it all came from one fight. My assumption is that his physical condition resulted from repeated blows to the head over time."[9]

In addition to his declining health, Ali had to deal with the breakup of his third marriage. He and wife Veronica simply found their lives moving in different directions. In September 1985, the pair filed for divorce. The statement said that "the decision to dissolve the marriage was mutually agreed upon by Muhammad and Veronica" and that "their deep friendship remains intact."[10] Still, Muhammad was sad to see the marriage ending and to realize that daughters Hana and Laila would be moving out, too.

> **In addition to his declining health, Ali had to deal with the breakup of his third marriage.**

The divorce became final in the summer of 1986, and Ali gave his ex-wife an extremely generous settlement. In the end, according to some sources, Veronica ended up coming out of the divorce with more money than her former husband.[11]

Not long after the divorce from Veronica, Ali asked Lonnie to marry him. It was hardly a romantic proposal. Actually, recalls Lonnie, he said, "Why don't you see if you can get a marriage license, and we'll get married in Louisville."[12]

Almost from the time he married Lonnie, Ali's life

Muhammad Ali in 1993 with his wife Lonnie, and their adopted son, Asaad.

started to improve. He was happy when he was with her. Also, his medical condition seemed to have stabilized somewhat. Soon the couple bought a farm in Berrien, Michigan. Ali loved life on the farm. He enjoyed bringing his family together there. "We would fly all of my children to the farm for summers," he said. "We called this time Camp Lonnie because she did all the work, organizing and keeping it interesting. This was not an easy task; it took a lot of time and energy. But Lonnie did it because she knew how much it meant to me."[13]

Gradually, Ali adjusted to his new lifestyle and his physical limitations. He spent much of his time praying, studying the Qur'an, signing autographs, and entertaining the frequent visitors who came to the house. They wanted to meet one of the most famous people in the world.

Often Ali entertained some of his visitors with magic tricks. He made himself appear to levitate. He made a handkerchief seem to disappear. Then, because Muslims are not supposed to deceive people, he would explain how he performed the tricks.

"Muhammad has an open-door policy," Lonnie said. "Whoever comes to the door, no matter what time it is . . . he invites them in. They come from all over the world, not to mention every corner of the United States. I don't know what they're doing here, but they wind up at our front door and Muhammad invites them in."[14]

Ali's days at home revolved around a set routine. Each morning he got up early and prayed. As a devout Muslim, he observed five such prayer sessions daily. In between prayer sessions, he studied the Qur'an. He also spent a lot of time signing autographs. Indeed, it was said that he gave away more than one hundred thousand autographs a year.[15]

After his hectic life as a boxer, Ali appreciated the quiet of his farm. "Boxing was good to me while it lasted," he said, "but it was only a start to what I want to accomplish in life. Here on the farm, I can rest up for my true mission—loving people and spreading the word of God."[16]

Sadness arrived as the 1980s wound down, with the death of Ali's friend Drew Bundini Brown, who was an assistant trainer and cornerman to Ali. Then, Ali's father died in February 1990. The two had not been close for a number of years. Still, his father's death affected him deeply.

Ali continued traveling. In 1990, he met Nelson Mandela, who had worked to end South Africa's apartheid, the system which kept whites and blacks separated and gave whites control of economic and political power. He later became president of South Africa.

Ali also met Mother Teresa, a Catholic nun who worked with poor and sick people in India. He became her friend. She took him to a hospital, where he visited with sick children.

Later that year, he made a controversial trip that reinforced his image of following his beliefs regardless of what others thought. On August 2, 1990, Iraq invaded neighboring Kuwait. This gave Iraq and its leader, dictator Saddam Hussein, control of a large percentage of the world's oil supply. Furthermore, the United States feared that Iraq would next try to invade Saudia Arabia and its rich store of oil. The United States, with support of the United Nations, demanded unsuccessfully that Iraq leave Kuwait. Iraq also took hostage some three hundred Americans who were working in Kuwait. It began to appear that the United States would go to war with Iraq.

During the 1990s, Ali's popularity continued to grow.

In November 1990, Ali traveled to Iraq. He hoped there was something he could do to help prevent war

from breaking out. Many people, including some of
Ali's best friends, feared that the trip would backfire.
They thought Hussein would use the publicity to his
advantage. They feared that Ali would look bad. Indeed,
many people were offended at photos of Ali embracing
the Iraqi leader.

However, Ali did persuade Hussein to release fifteen
of the hostages. One of these hostages, Harry Brill-
Edwards, was very ill. "I suppose what impressed me
most about Ali was the way he cared for everyone,"
said Brill-Edwards. "He had a kind word or gesture for
absolutely every person he saw."[17]

Furthermore, Ali had risked his own health to make
the trip. When he left on his mission, he had enough of
his Parkinson's medicine for five days. The trip lasted
two weeks. He endangered his own health because he
believed that what he was doing was right.[18]

During the 1990s, Ali's popularity continued to
grow. In 1991, Thomas Hauser published his bestselling
biography, *Muhammad Ali: His Life and Times*. It
included interviews with some two hundred people,
ranging from family members to boxers to notable
people from around the world. It brought Ali's life story
to a whole new generation of people.

In 1992, a galaxy of stars joined in a television event
to celebrate Ali's fiftieth birthday. Participants included
actors such as Arnold Schwarzenegger, Sylvester
Stallone, and Dustin Hoffman; singers Ella Fitzgerald,
Little Richard, and Diana Ross; basketball star Magic
Johnson; and sports commentator Howard Cosell.

Cosell was nearly as brash as Ali. The two had kept up a running banter for nearly three decades. They often kidded each other. On this occasion, however, Cosell offered solemn praise, noting that, "You are exactly who you said you are. You never wavered. You are free to be who you wanted to be. I love you." Ali was visibly moved as he listened to this tribute from his old friend.[19]

And while many people seemed concerned about his health, Ali said he was fine and that he was ready for whatever might lie ahead. "The first 50 years of my life were a preparation for the next 50 years," he said in a telephone interview.[20]

Despite his continuing health problems, the 1990s turned out to be a great decade for Ali. For one thing, he and Lonnie adopted a little boy named Asaad. Ali doted on Asaad. He had always regretted not spending more time with his other children. He enjoyed having the chance for a fresh start with Asaad. He also maintained closer ties with his eight other children.

Meanwhile, the legend of Ali continued to grow. In 1996, millions of people around the world watched as Ali, his hands trembling due to his Parkinson's syndrome symptoms, lit the Olympic flame for the Summer Olympics in Atlanta. The dramatic ceremony, which moved many to tears, reminded a generation of fans that Ali remained one of the most recognizable figures in the entire world. The event also brought him recognition from a new generation.

NBC commentator Bob Costas put it this way,

In 1996, Muhammad Ali lit the
Olympic flame for the Summer
Olympic games in Atlanta, Georgia.

"Once the most dynamic figure in sports, a gregarious man now trapped inside that mask created by Parkinson's syndrome, so in one sense a poignant figure, but look at him, still a great, great presence, still exuding nobility and stature. And the response he evokes is part affection, part excitement, but especially respect. What a moment!"[21]

What did that moment mean to him? He shared his thoughts in an interview in *Reader's Digest* with his friend Howard Bingham. "It showed that people in the past didn't hold it against me because here I am rejecting the Vietnam War, joining the Islamic religion, and then, of all people, raising the flag," he said. "They were thinking of me to light the Olympic flame, so that was a good thing."[22]

At halftime of the gold-medal basketball game of that same Olympics, the president of the International Olympic Committee presented Ali with a replacement gold medal for the one he lost from his 1960 triumph. Ali proudly kissed the medal as the crowd roared and members of the American basketball "Dream Team," which included Michael Jordan and Shaquille O'Neal, congratulated him. Ali held up his hands, slowly turned as if to acknowledge everyone in the crowd, and then walked off the court to deafening applause.

That year also marked the release of *When We Were Kings*. This powerful documentary described the "Rumble in the Jungle" when Ali defeated George Foreman in Zaire. The film won an Academy Award for

Best Documentary Feature. It also won legions of new fans for Ali.

In 1999, Ali learned that his youngest daughter, Laila Ali, wished to pursue a boxing career. At first, Ali expressed concern about her decision. "Being a fighter isn't easy," he said. "What are you going to do when you get hit upside your head, get all dizzy, and don't know where you are? As my daughter, do you realize the pressure that'll be on you?"[23]

He asked her many more questions as well. She wondered if she would ever get his support. Finally he said, "Okay, come over here and show me your left jab." When she passed that test, she knew she had won him over.[24]

> "The first 50 years of my life were a preparation for the next 50 years."

Laila Ali established a successful boxing career and became the most famous of her famous father's offspring. As of 2008 she held a perfect 24-0 record. Like her father, she has held a world boxing championship. She has also participated in the television show *Dancing With the Stars* (she finished third), and she served as cohost of *American Gladiators* in 2008 with Hulk Hogan.

Muhammad Ali takes pride in Laila's achievements in the ring. But he also takes pride in all his children. "Because of the divorces and the way I lived, I wasn't really around to raise them," he said. "But they turned out good, all of them. None of them are into drugs; they live right. And whatever they need, I try to give it to them."[25]

After years of concern about his finances, Ali has been on more solid ground lately. He launched a company called Greatest of All Time (GOAT) to explore business ventures. And Lonnie watches over most of his business affairs.

In 2007, on his sixty-fifth birthday, Ali's company released a line of health food snacks aimed at the eighteen- to twenty-four-year-old age group. The snacks come in the shape of a boxing glove. Flavors include "Slammin' Salsa" and "Thrilla a Dill-A."

In December 1999, he was named the athlete of the century by *Sports Illustrated* and the BBC. The new millennium brought even more honors to Ali. The highly acclaimed film *Ali,* starring Will Smith, was released in 2001. Smith earned an Academy Award nomination for his portrayal of Ali. Smith also earned even higher praise—approval from Ali himself.

In September 2000, the United Nations named Ali a Messenger of Peace. He is one of just a handful of world figures to have held this post. Messengers of Peace are high-profile people who agree to help focus worldwide attention on the work of the United Nations.

"Over the years Mr. Ali has been a relentless advocate for people in need and a significant humanitarian actor in the developing world, supporting relief and development initiatives and hand-delivering food and medical supplies to hospitals, street children and orphanages in Africa and Asia," according to the Messengers of Peace webpage.[26]

In that capacity and as a concerned citizen, Ali had

Actor Will Smith portrayed Muhammad Ali in a 2001 movie called *Ali*.

been involved in relief missions to countries in Africa, Asia, and the Caribbean. In 1998, he went on a humanitarian mission to deliver medicine and medical equipment to Cuba. In 2002, he traveled to Afghanistan to raise awareness of the country's needs and the United Nations' work there.

Ali also worked to make life better for other boxers. In 2000, Congress passed the Muhammad Ali Boxing Reform Act. The act is designed to protect professional boxers by preventing exploitative, oppressive, and unethical business practices. It also called for assisting state boxing commissions in having better public oversight of the sport.

In addition, Ali has been involved in many other

humanitarian projects. For example, his Celebrity Fight Night has raised more than $45 million for the Muhammad Ali Parkinson Center at Barrow Neurological Institute. In May 2005, he traveled to San Antonio, Texas, for the presentation of the READ 180 All-Star Awards at the annual convention of the International Reading Association. There he congratulated the winners, pretending to box with some of them.

The READ 180 program, produced by children's publisher Scholastic Inc., aims to help older students who struggle with reading. "Having struggled with my own dyslexia, I am especially happy to honor students who overcame their own personal challenges to become accomplished readers," Ali said.[27]

In addition, Ali and Peter Georgi founded the Los Angeles Children's General Assembly, which is based in Los Angeles. This United Nations-authorized organization is designed to allow children to participate in promoting world peace, environmental healing, sustainable development, education, and many other pressing issues.

In 2007, the Gandhi Foundation of the United States nominated Ali and Georgi for the Nobel Peace Prize for their work on this project. "You cannot find a better candidate than Muhammad Ali for the Nobel Peace Prize," said Subash Razdan, chairman of the Gandhi Foundation USA. "In the words of Mahatma Gandhi, if we want world peace, we must begin with children and Muhammad Ali made history when he got a voice to our children through the United Nations."[28]

In 2005, Laila Ali poses with her father after she won a boxing match.

In 2005, Ali received the prestigious Presidential Medal of Freedom. His citation read as follows:

> One of the greatest athletes of all time, Muhammad Ali produced some of America's most lasting sports memories, from winning the Gold Medal at the 1960 Summer Olympics to carrying the Olympic torch at the 1996 Summer Olympics. As the first three-time heavyweight boxing champion of the world, he thrilled, entertained, and inspired us. His deep commitment to equal justice and peace has touched people around the world. The United States honors Muhammad Ali for his lifetime of achievement and for his principled service to mankind.[29]

At the White House ceremony, President George W. Bush embraced Ali and pretended to box with him. Ali simply smiled.

Over the years, the effects of Parkinson's have reduced Ali's ability to walk and to speak. Still, he keeps busy, traveling as much as he can. He takes special pride in his humanitarian work. The crowning jewel of this work is the Muhammad Ali Center, which opened in Louisville on November 19, 2005. Fans from around the world, including actors Brad Pitt and Jim Carrey and former U.S. president Bill Clinton, attended the grand opening ceremony. "You thrilled us as a fighter and you inspired us even more as a force for peace and reconciliation, understanding and respect," Clinton said. "As your body slowed down, your heart speeded up."[30]

The $80-million museum features a variety of exhibitions reflecting Ali's six values: respect, confidence, conviction, dedication, giving, and spirituality. Interactive pavilions and multimedia presentations tell Ali's story. Visitors can try their hand at shadowboxing with the champ or working on the speed bag in an exhibit that recreates Ali's Deer Lake Training Camp. They can relive the moment when Ali lit the Olympic flame in 1996 and see exhibits offering historical contexts—both in terms of sports and society at large—for Ali's accomplishments.

Ali simply smiled.

The Muhammad Ali Center has received a 5-Star Award for Best New Attraction from the North American Travel Journalists Association and a "Best Places" award from *Pathfinders Travel Magazine*. It seems to be fulfilling its primary mission: To preserve and share the legacy and ideals of Muhammad Ali, to promote respect, hope and understanding, and to inspire adults and children everywhere to be as great as they can be.[31]

Another milestone came in 2007 when Ali celebrated his sixty-fifth birthday. A steady stream of people came to the Muhammad Ali Center. Many had their pictures taken holding a sign wishing him a happy birthday. Ali himself celebrated quietly with Lonnie at their residence in Scottsdale, Arizona. That evening, he watched an old friend, comedian Billy Crystal, perform at Arizona State University. Ali joined Crystal on stage, where he received a standing ovation.

Having moved from their farm in Berrien Springs, Ali and Lonnie spend most of their time these days in

Arizona. They also own a house in Jefferson County, Kentucky, near Ali's hometown of Louisville. Although Ali does not travel as much as he once did, he still shows up for various events and functions.

For instance, in September 2008, Louisville hosted the Ryder Cup, a golfing competition that matches a team of top golfers from Europe against a team from the United States. Before the matches began, Ali hosted a reception at the Muhammad Ali Center. According to reporter Dave Perkins of the *Toronto Star,* Ali needed help getting up and down the two stairs to the podium. Because he has difficulty speaking, his wife, Lonnie, did most of the talking.

> **"My greatest privilege in life was becoming a messenger of peace and love."**

Despite this, said Perkins, "Ali's entrance is one long standing ovation" as the crowd honors "the magnetic figure who changed the sports world, if not the world itself, more than 40 years ago."[32]

Later, Ali showed up on the last practice day to meet the players and pose for photographs. European captain Nick Faldo, known for his calm demeanor on the golf course, had tears in his eyes. "Meeting him was just an incredible moment," he said. Meanwhile, American captain Paul Azinger told Ali that he remembered watching Ali's first fight with Ken Norton as a youngster. That was the fight where Ali fought most of the fight with a broken jaw. "And I told him that was an inspiration for me to never quit, no matter what,"

Azinger said. "It was a great privilege to sit next to a great man."[33]

These days Ali is also a humble person. The man who once "shook up the world" with his brash ways now prizes the quiet things in life—his wife, his children and grandchildren, his religion. "My greatest accomplishments in life were achieved outside the ring," he said, "and my greatest privilege in life was becoming a messenger of peace and love. Because there is nothing as great as working for God."[34]

Chapter 10

Living Legacy

At the height of his popularity in the 1970s,
Muhammad Ali was arguably the most famous person
in the entire world. Even today, more than a quarter
century after his last fight, his name and face draw
instant recognition in almost any corner of the world.

During his years as a fighter—whether pummeling
opponents in the ring or battling the establishment
outside of it—Muhammad Ali seemed larger than life.
Millions loved him for his brash personality and dazzling
skills. Others resented his cockiness and his outspoken
criticism of the Vietnam War. But love him or hate him,
he stirred emotions in people in a way that no one
else could.

"He was bigger than boxing; he was bigger than
sports," said baseball slugger Reggie Jackson, who was
himself a brash, larger-than-life figure. "When people
call Muhammad Ali 'the greatest,' they know what
they're talking about."[1]

And where does Ali rank in the all-time annals of boxing? Ali's own heavyweight rankings of all time place himself first, Jack Johnson second, and Joe Louis in third place.[2]

In a 1998 ranking, *Ring Magazine* agreed, placing him atop the greatest heavyweights from all eras. ESPN.com named him the second greatest fighter in boxing history at any weight level, behind only Sugar Ray Robinson.[3]

Furthermore, Ali's longtime trainer, Angelo Dundee, reminds us that Ali lost three and a half of his prime boxing years while he was suspended from the sport for draft evasion. "We never saw him at his peak," Dundee says.[4]

Writer Robert Lipsyte described Ali as "always accessible, always friendly, always basically decent and helpful. And finally, after many years, the world at large saw him that way. Even people who had once thought he was awful let go of their emotional baggage and accepted him for what he was."[5]

"Muhammad is one of the few Americans, and certainly the first American athlete ever, to transcend the borders of this country and become an international hero," added sportswriter Bert Sugar. "He was the greatest sports hero of all time."[6]

But he was more than just a sports hero. The true magic of Ali is that his legend continued to grow even after he retired from boxing. His ongoing humanitarianism earned him accolades throughout the world.

After Ali's boxing career ended, Parkinson's syndrome ravaged his once magnificent body. His hands,

In 2009, Muhammad Ali sits on stage during a health and nutrition conference. Ali continues to be an inspiration to people everywhere.

once fast as lightning, now trembled. His once-slick speech was now slurred and slow. Oddly, his health struggles contributed to making him almost universally beloved. Even those who had not appreciated him as a fighter admired the grace and courage with which he now faced his physical challenges.

Bestselling author Alex Haley put it this way: "You know, there's a reality for anybody who studies history. And that is that ninety-nine-point-nine-nine-nine percent of the people who live will be totally forgotten a hundred years after they die. And of those who are remembered, only a small proportion will have made a significant and positive impact upon the world. But I think Ali will be one of those people."[7]

And how does Ali himself want to be remembered? "I would like to be remembered as a man who won the heavyweight title three times, who was humorous, and who treated everyone right. As a man who never looked down on those who looked up to him, and who helped as many people as he could. As a man who stood up for his beliefs no matter what. As a man who tried to unite all humankind through faith and love," he says. "And if all that's too much, then I guess I'd settle for being remembered only as a great boxer who became a leader and a champion of his people. And I wouldn't even mind if folks forgot how pretty I was."[8]

Chronology

1942—Cassius Marcellus Clay, Jr., is born on January 17 in Louisville, Kentucky.

1945—World War II ends.

1954—Begins taking boxing lessons after his bike is stolen; wins his first amateur bout.

1955—Wins novice boxing title in Louisville, Kentucky.

1959—Wins National AAU Light Heavyweight Championship for first of two consecutive years.

1960—Graduates high school near the bottom of his class; wins Olympic gold medal in light heavyweight division in Rome, Italy; wins first professional fight against Tunney Hunsaker; begins training with Angelo Dundee in Miami, Florida.

1961—Wins first main-event bout against Donnie Freeman; begins habit of predicting in which round he will win a fight.

1962—Fights for the first time in Madison Square Garden; defeats former heavyweight champion Archie Moore.

1963—Fights outside the United States for the first time, beating British heavyweight champion Henry Cooper; signs in November to meet Sonny Liston for the world heavyweight championship the following year.

1964—Defeats Sonny Liston to win the heavyweight crown on February 25; announces that he is a Muslim; takes new Muslim name of Muhammad Ali; makes a monthlong trip to Africa; marries Sonji Roi on August 14; signs for a rematch with Sonny Liston, but the fight is postponed after Ali has emergency hernia surgery.

1965—Wins rematch with Sonny Liston on May 25 with a "phantom punch"; defeats former champion Floyd Patterson on November 22.

1966—Requests deferment from being drafted into the armed service for the Vietnam War, but the request is denied; divorces Sonji Roi; names Herbert Muhammad as his new manager; defends his crown several times.

1967—Refuses to be inducted into the U.S. armed forces and is stripped of his boxing license and heavyweight championship; is indicted by a federal grand jury and is released on bail, pending appeal; marries seventeen-year-old Belinda Boyd on August 17.

1968—Welcomes birth of first child, daughter Maryum; loses appeal of his draft case in Appeals Court.

1969—Appears in the Broadway show *Big Time Buck White*.

1970—Welcomes twin daughters Rasheeda and Jemillah; U.S. Supreme Court decrees that conscientious objector status can be allowed on religious grounds alone, which strengthens Ali's case and sets up his return to the ring; returns to the ring with victories against Jerry Quarry and Oscar Bonavena.

1971—Loses classic bout with Joe Frazier in March; wins Supreme Court ruling that causes all charges against him to be dropped; wins three matches on his comeback trail.

1972—Welcomes son Muhammad, Jr.; fights six bouts during the course of the year, winning all six.

1973—Suffers a broken jaw and loses a fight against Ken Norton; wins rematch later in the year, along with two other bouts.

1974—Wins rematch with Joe Frazier; regains heavyweight title by beating George Foreman in the "Rumble in the Jungle" in Zaire; accepts invitation from President Gerald Ford to visit the White House.

1975—Successfully defends title four times, including "The Thrilla in Manila" over Joe Frazier; publishes autobiography, *The Greatest*.

1976—Welcomes arrival of daughter Hana, born to Ali's mistress, Veronica Porsche; successfully defends title four times, including a third bout with Ken Norton; battles to an embarrassing draw with professional wrestler Antonio Inoki in a boxing/wrestling match.

1977—Welcomes daughter Laila; divorces Belinda Ali and marries Veronica Porsche; successfully defends title twice, including a hard-fought bout against Earnie Shavers.

1978—Loses title to Leon Spinks and then regains it in a rematch, becoming the first three-time champion in history.

1979—Announces retirement from boxing; stars in television miniseries *Freedom Road*.

1980—Returns to boxing and loses badly to Larry Holmes.

1981—Loses final bout of his career to Trevor Berbick.

1984—Receives diagnosis of Parkinson's syndrome, explaining the tremors, slurred speech, fatigue, and other symptoms he has been suffering.

1986—Divorces Veronica Porsche; marries Yolanda "Lonnie" Williams.

1990—Travels to Iraq on peace mission prior to the beginning of the Gulf War; succeeds in securing release of fifteen Americans held hostage in Iraq.

1992—Adopts son, Asaad.

1996—Lights Olympic flame at the Summer Olympics in Atlanta; enjoys release of *When We Were Kings,* Academy Award-winning documentary about the "Rumble in the Jungle."

1999—Watches daughter Laila begin a professional boxing career; is named athlete of the century by *Sports Illustrated* and the BBC.

2000—Is named a Messenger of Peace by the United Nations; celebrates passage by the U.S. Congress of the Muhammad Ali Boxing Reform Act, designed to protect boxers from exploitation.

2001—Enjoys release of film biography *Ali,* starring Will Smith.

2005—Celebrates opening of Muhammad Ali Center in Louisville, Kentucky; receives Presidential Medal of Freedom from President George W. Bush.

2007—Celebrates sixty-fifth birthday; nominated for a Nobel Peace Prize.

2008—Attends the opening of the Ryder Cup golf competition in Louisville, inspiring both the American and European teams.

Glossary

abolitionist—One who wishes to do away with something.

accolades—Praise.

bout—A contest or match, as in boxing.

brash—Tactless or rash; it can also mean highly spirited in an irreverent way.

civil rights movement—A movement in the United States to gain equal rights for African Americans.

confiscated—Taken away, removed.

conscientious objector—A person who refuses to serve in the armed forces for moral or religious reasons.

controversy—A public dispute caused by a difference of opinion.

deferment—A temporary exemption from being inducted into military service; deferments can be offered for a variety of reasons.

disproportionate—Out of line with the proportion or number one would expect.

entourage—A group of people who travel with someone of importance.

evasion—The act of escaping, avoiding, or getting away from something or someone.

exile—To expel or banish.

humanitarian—Concerned with the welfare of the entire human race.

indicted—Formally accused of a crime.

inducted—Admitted as a member; often used in connection with being taken into military service.

integration—The act of mixing or bringing parts together as a whole; often used in connection with integrating races or religions.

knockout—In boxing, a situation where a fighter is knocked down and cannot get back up by the count of ten.

mismatch—In boxing, a bout in which one fighter is far superior to the other.

Parkinson's syndrome—A set of symptoms similar to those of Parkinson's disease, which may include tremors, slurred speech, and lack of steadiness when walking.

poignant—Affecting the emotions, often causing sadness.

prejudice—Having an unfavorable opinion about someone or something that is not based on fact but on prior attitudes; prejudice often occurs based on race, religion, or national origin.

segregation—The act of separating or keeping apart; especially used in the sense of keeping races separate.

separatism—A belief in keeping people or groups separate from each other.

simulate—To create a likeness or model of a situation or event.

surveillance—The act of keeping watch over something or someone, often done secretly.

technical knockout—A situation in boxing where the bout is stopped because a fighter is judged unable to continue by the referee, the attending physician, or the people in the boxer's corner.

transcend—To go beyond.

Chapter Notes

Chapter 1. Taking a Stand

1. Thomas Hauser, *Muhammad Ali: His Life and Times* (New York: Simon & Schuster, 1991), p. 169.
2. Ibid., pp. 454–455.
3. John Stravinsky, *Muhammad Ali* (New York: Park Lane Press, 1997), p. 89.
4. Hauser, p. 203.
5. Ibid., p. 171.

Chapter 2. It Began With a Bike

1. Muhammad Ali with Richard Durham, *The Greatest: My Own Story* (New York: Random House, 1975), p. 34.
2. Thomas Hauser, *Muhammad Ali: His Life and Times* (New York: Simon & Schuster, 1991), p. 15.
3. Ibid., p. 16.
4. Muhammad Ali, with Hana Yasmeen Ali, *The Soul of a Butterfly: Reflections on Life's Journey* (New York: Simon & Schuster, 2004), p. 4.
5. Hauser, pp. 14–15.
6. Muhammad Ali, with Hana Yasmeen Ali, pp. 5–6.
7. Hauser, p. 16.
8. José Torres and Bert Randolph Sugar, *Sting Like a Bee: The Muhammad Ali Story* (New York: Abelard-Schuman Limited, 1971), p. 84.
9. Hauser, p. 18.
10. Muhammad Ali, with Hana Yasmeen Ali, p. 18.
11. Hauser, p. 18.

12. Ibid., p. 19,
13. Ibid., p. 19.
14. Felix Dennis and Don Atyeo, *Muhammad Ali: The Glory Years* (New York: Hyperion, 2003), p. 32.
15. Hauser, p. 19.
16. John Stravinsky, *Muhammad Ali* (New York: Park Lane Press, 1997), p. 14.
17. Muhammad Ali, with Hana Yasmeen Ali, p. 26.
18. David Remnick, *King of the World* (New York: Random House, 1998), p. 95.
19. Ibid., p. 88.
20. Hauser, p. 20.
21. Ibid., p. 21.
22. Martin Kane, "Ready to Go in Rome," *Sports Illustrated*, August 29, 1960, p. 12.
23. Muhammad Ali, with Hana Yasmeen Ali, p. 28.

Chapter 3. Golden Boy Turns Pro

1. David Maraniss, "When Worlds Collided," *Sports Illustrated*, May 27, 2008, p. 59.
2. Muhammad Ali with Hana Yasmeen Ali, *The Soul of a Butterfly: Reflections on Life's Journey* (New York: Simon & Schuster, 2004), p. 34.
3. Thomas Hauser, *Muhammad Ali: His Life and Times* (New York: Simon & Schuster, 1991), p. 26.
4. Ibid., p. 24.
5. Felix Dennis and Don Atyeo, *Muhammad Ali: The Glory Years* (New York: Hyperion, 2003), p. 44.
6. Maraniss, p. 60.
7. Muhammad Ali with Richard Durham, *The Greatest* (New York: Random House, 1976), p. 70.
8. Muhammad Ali, with Hana Yasmeen Ali, *The Soul of a Butterfly*, p. 40.

9. John Stravinsky, *Muhammad Ali* (New York: Park Lane Press/Random House, 1997), p. 24.

10. Hauser, p. 30.

11. Ibid., pp. 30–31.

12. José Torres and Bert Randolph Sugar, *Sting Like a Bee: The Muhammad Ali Story* (New York: Contemporary Books, 2002), p. 98.

13. Hauser, p. 31.

14. Stephen Brunt, *Facing Ali* (Guilford, CT: The Lyons Press, 2002), p. 22.

15. Dennis and Atyeo, p. 50.

16. Hauser, p. 34.

17. Ibid., p. 35.

18. Dennis and Atyeo, p. 54.

19. David Remnick, *King of the World* (New York: Random House, 1998), 117.

20. Hauser, p. 36.

21. Dennis and Atyeo, p. 58.

22. John Capouya, "King Strut," *Sports Illustrated*, December 12, 2005, <http://vault.sportsillustrated. cnn.com/vault/article/magazine/MAG1114630/ index.htm> (September 15, 2008).

23. Hauser, p. 39.

24. Ibid., p. 41.

25. Dennis and Atyeo, p. 62.

26. Hauser, p. 49.

27. Ibid., p. 54.

Chapter 4. **The Greatest**

1. David Remnick, *King of the World* (New York: Random House, 1998), p. 55.

2. Thomas Hauser, *Muhammad Ali: His Life and Times* (New York: Simon & Schuster, 1991), p. 59

3. Remnick, p. 77.

4. José Torres and Bert Randolph Sugar, *Sting Like a Bee: The Muhammad Ali Story* (New York: Contemporary Books/McGraw-Hill, 2002), p. 121.

5. Ibid., p. 123.

6. Felix Dennis and Don Atyeo, *Muhammad Ali: The Glory Years* (New York: Hyperion, 2003), p. 90.

7. Hauser, p. 60.

8. Ibid., p. 60.

9. Remnick, pp. 148–149.

10. Ibid., p. 147.

11. The "I Have a Dream" Speech, U.S. Constitution Online website <http://www. usconstitution.net/dream.html> (September 10, 2008).

12. Ibid.

13. "God's Judgement of White America (The Chickens Come Home to Roost)" speech from December 4, 1963, *Malcolm-x.org*, <http://www.malcolm-x.org/speeches/spc_120463.htm> (January 16, 2009).

14. Muhammad Ali with Hana Yasmeen Ali, *The Soul of a Butterfly: Reflections on Life's Journey* (New York: Simon & Schuster, 2004), p. 76.

15. Dennis and Atyeo, p. 120.

16. Bob Spitz, *The Beatles: The Biography* (New York: Little, Brown and Company, 2005), p. 484.

17. Muhammad Ali, with Richard Durham, *The Greatest: My Own Story* (New York: Random House, 1975), pp. 115–116.

18. Remnick, p. 181.

19. Muhammad Ali with Richard Durham, pp. 115–116.

20. Ibid., p. 117.

21. Ibid., p. 118.
22. Ferdie Pacheco, *Muhammad Ali: A View from the Corner* (New York: Birch Lane Press/Carol Publishing Group, 1992), p. 78.
23. Dennis and Atyeo, p. 106.
24. Remnick, p. 200.

Chapter 5. The Legend Grows

1. Thomas Hauser, *Muhammad Ali: His Life and Times* (New York: Simon & Schuster, 1991), p. 82.
2. David Remnick, *King of the World* (New York: Random House, 1998), p. 210.
3. Elliot Gorn, *Muhammad Ali: The People's Champ* (Champaign, Ill.: University of Illinois Press, 1998) p. 129.
4. Felix Dennis and Don Atyeo, *Muhammad Ali: The Glory Years* (New York: Hyperion, 2003), p. 126.
5. Remnick, p. 209.
6. Hauser, p. 108.
7. Jack Cashill, *Sucker Punch* (Nashville, Tennessee: Nelson Current, 2006), p. 74.
8. Muhammad Ali with Hana Yasmeen Ali, *The Soul of a Butterfly: Reflections on Life's Journey* (New York: Simon & Schuster, 2004), p. 85.
9. Hauser, p. 115.
10. Ibid., p. 116.
11. Ibid., p. 129.
12. Ibid., p. 130.
13. Ferdie Pacheco, *Muhammad Ali: A View from the Corner* (New York: Birch Lane Press/Carol Publishing Group, 1992), p. 81.
14. Ibid., p. 81.
15. Remnick, p. 239.

16. Muhammad Ali with Richard Durham, *The Greatest* (New York: Random House, 1975), p. 122.
17. Hauser, p. 127.
18. Pacheco, p. 84.
19. Hauser, p. 127.
20. Pacheco, pp. 84–86.
21. "Muhammad Ali vs. Sonny Liston 1965," *YouTube*, n.d., <http://www.youtube.com/watch?v=uzWynvBLJ4I&feature=related> (September 13, 2008).
22. José Torres and Bert Randolph Sugar, *Sting Like a Bee: The Muhammad Ali Story* (New York: Contemporary Books/McGraw-Hill, 2002), p. 143.
23. Hauser, p. 133.
24. Ibid., p. 139.
25. Ibid., p. 139.
26. John Stravinsky, *Muhammad Ali: A Biography* (New York: Park Lane Press/Random, 1997), p. 66.
27. Dennis and Atyeo, p. 138.

Chapter 6. **Living in Exile**

1. Felix Dennis and Don Atyeo, *Muhammad Ali: The Glory Years* (New York: Hyperion, 2003), p. 138.
2. Ibid., p. 138.
3. José Torres and Bert Randolph Sugar, *Sting Like a Bee* (New York: Contemporary Books/McGraw-Hill, 2002), p. 147.
4. Thomas Hauser, *Muhammad Ali: His Life and Times* (New York: Simon & Schuster, 1991), p. 143.
5. Muhammad Ali with Richard Durham, *The Greatest: My Own Story* (New York: Random House, 1975), p. 129.
6. Hauser, p. 145.

7. Torres, p. 151.

8. Hauser, p. 154.

9. Ann Oliver and Paul Simpson, Editors, *The Rough Guide to Muhammad Ali* (London: Haymarket Customer Publishing, 2004), p. 48.

10. Hauser, p. 160.

11. Dennis and Atyeo, p. 150.

12. Hauser, p. 169.

13. John Stravinsky, Muhammad Ali (New York: Park Lane Press/Random House, 1977), p. 81.

14. Hauser, p. 180.

15. Ibid., p. 180.

16. Hauser, p. 184.

17. Muhammad Ali with Hana Yasmeen Ali, *The Soul of a Butterfly: Reflections on Life's Journey* (New York: Simon & Schuster, 2004), p. 98.

18. Hauser, p. 192.

19. Stravinsky, p. 91.

20. Ibid., p. 91.

21. Jack Cashill, *Sucker Punch* (Nashville, Tennessee: Nelson Current), p. 118.

22. Hauser, p. 203.

23. Dennis and Atyeo, p. 160.

24. "Playboy Interview: Muhammad Ali." Reprinted in condensed form in *The Muhammad Ali Reader*, edited by Gerald Early (Hopewell, New Jersey: The Ecco Press, 1998), p. 154.

25. Ibid., p. 155.

26. Hauser, p. 207.

Chapter 7. Epic Battles

1. Thomas Hauser, *Muhammad Ali: His Life and Times* (New York: Simon & Schuster, 1991), p. 208.

2. John Stravinsky, *Muhammad Ali* (New York: Park Lane Press/Random House, 1997) p. 94.

3. Ann Oliver and Paul Simpson, Editors, *The Rough Guide to Muhammad Ali* (New York: Haymarket Customer Publishing, 2004), p. 133.

4. Hauser, p. 219.

5. José Torres, *Sting Like a Bee: The Muhammad Ali Story* (New York: Contemporary Books, McGraw-Hill), p. 212.

6. Muhammad Ali with Richard Durham, *The Greatest: My Own Story* (New York: Random House, 1975), p. 358.

7. Ferdie Pacheco, *Muhammad Ali: A View from the Corner* (New York: Birch Lane Press/Carol Publishing Group, 1992), p. 106.

8. "Clay, aka Ali v. United States 1966–1971, African-American Involvement in the Vietnam War," n.d., <http: www.aavw.org/protest/ali_alivus_abstract08.html> (September 15, 2008).

9. Ibid.

10. Stravinsky, p. 105.

11. Pacheco, p. 111.

12. Hauser, p. 253.

13. Pacheco, p. 111.

14. Ibid, p. 115.

15. Oliver and Simpson, Editors, p. 69.

16. Hauser, p. 260.

17. Ibid., p. 269.

18. Muhammad Ali with Richard Durham, p. 400.

19. Hauser, p. 274.

20. Muhammad Ali with Richard Durham, p. 413.

21. Stephen Brunt, *Facing Ali: 15 Fighters, 15 Stories* (Guilford, Connecticut: The Lyons Press, 2002), p. 197.

22. Hauser, pp. 300–301.

23. Ibid., p. 310.

24. Oliver and Simpson, Editors, p. 158.

25. Mark Kram, "Lawdy, Lawdy, He's Great," *Sports Illustrated*, October 13, 1975, p. 22.

26. Ibid., p. 22.

27. Hauser, p. 326.

Chapter 8. Falling Star

1. Thomas Hauser, *Muhammad Ali: His Life and Times* (New York: Simon & Schuster, 1991), p. 342.

2. Vincent Canby, "Movie Review: *Muhammad Ali, The Greatest 1964–74*", *The New York Times*, November 23, 1990, <http://movies.nytimes.com/movie/review?res=9C0CE1DA123FF930A15752C1A966958260> (September 18, 2008).

3. Stephen Brunt, *Facing Ali: 15 Fighters, 15 Stories* (Guilford, Connecticut: The Lyons Press, 2002), p. 272.

4. Hauser, pp. 348–349.

5. Ferdie Pacheco, *Muhammad Ali: A View from the Corner* (New York: Birch Lane Press/Carol Publishing Group, 1992), p. 151.

6. Ibid., p. 151.

7. Felix Dennis and Don Atyeo, *Muhammad Ali: The Glory Years* (New York: Hyperion, 2003), p. 254.

8. Ann Oliver and Paul Simpson, Editors, *The Rough Guide to Muhammad Ali* (New York: Haymarket Customer Publishing, 2004), p. 164.

9. Hauser, p. 353.

10. Pat Putnam, "The Old Lion Eyes Leon, "*Sports Illustrated*, September 11, 1978, p. 22.

11. Hauser, p. 361.

12. Ibid., p. 363.

13. Dennis and Atyeo, p. 260.

14. John Stravinsky, *Muhammad Ali* (New York: Park Lane Press/Random House, 1997) p. 145.

15. Hauser, p. 400.

16. Ibid., p. 405.

17. Brunt, p. 290.

18. Hauser, p. 412.

19. Ibid., pp. 412–413.

20. Ibid., p. 429.

21. William Nack, "Not With a Bang But a Whisper," *Sports Illustrated*, December 21, 1981, p. 29.

Chapter 9. **The Legend Lives On**

1. Thomas Hauser, *Muhammad Ali: His Life and Times* (New York: Simon & Schuster, 1991), p. 431.

2. Muhammad Ali with Hana Yasmeen Ali, *The Soul of Butterfly: Reflections on Life's Journey* (New York: Simon & Schuster, 2004), p. 168.

3. Felix Dennis and Don Atyeo, *Muhammad Ali: The Glory Years* (New York: Hyperion, 2003), p. 268.

4. Ibid., p. 268.

5. Hauser, p. 469.

6. Ibid., p. 431.

7. AP report, "Neurologist confirmed Ali's damage in '80," Frederick, Maryland, *News*, September 21, <http://www.newspaperararchive.com> (September 16, 2008).

8. Ferdie Pacheco, *Muhammad Ali: A View from the Corner* (New York: Birch Lane Press/Carol Publishing Group, 1992), p. 202.

9. Hauser, p. 492.

10. Dennis and Atyeo, p. 270.

11. Ibid., p. 270.

12. Hauser, p. 470.

13. Muhammad Ali with Hana Yasmeen Ali, p. 166.

14. Hauser, p. 474.

15. Ibid., p. 484.

16. Ibid., p. 466.

17. Hauser, p. 483.

18. Thomas Hauser, *The Lost Legacy of Muhammad Ali* (Toronto, Ontario: Sports Media Publishing, 2005), p. 52.

19. "Muhammad Ali 50th Birthday Tribute with Howard Cosell," *YouTube*, n.d., <http://www.youtube.com/watch?v=ZsK8QU-EAWo> (September 10, 2008).

20. "Ali's last opponent: time won't stand still," Lancaster, Pennsylvania, *Intelligencer/Record*, January 17, 1992, <http://www.newspaperarchive.com/PdfViewerTags.aspx?img=26409147&firstvisit=true&src=search&currentResult=2> (September 10, 2008).

21. "1996 Atlanta Opening Ceremonies: Lighting of the Cauldron," *YouTube*, <http://www.youtube.com/watch?v=5TalTzi64Sw> (September 1, 2008).

22. Howard Bingham, "Face to Face with Muhammad Ali," *Reader's Digest*, December 2001, <http://www.rd.com/your-america-inspiring-people-and-stories/face-to-face-with-muhammad-ali/article26496.html> (September 10, 2008).

23. Laila Ali with David Ritz, *Reach: Finding Strength, Spirit, and Personal Power* (New York: Hyperion, 2002), p. 141.

24. Ibid., p. 142.

25. Hauser, *Muhammad Ali: His Life and Times,* pp. 474–475.

26. United Nations Messengers of Peace webpage, n.d., <http://www.un.org/sg/mop/index.shtml> (September 10, 2008).

27. Scholastic, Inc., press release dated April 21, 2005, <http://www.teacher.scholastic.com/products/read180/pdfs/05_allstars.pdf> (July 4, 2008).

28. Suman Guha Mozumder, "U.S. Gandhi foundation nominates Muhammad Ali for Peace Nobel," *Rediff India Abroad*, September 13, 2007. <http://www.rediff.com/news/2007/sep/13nobel.htm> (September 10, 2008).

29. Citations for Recipients of the 2005 Presidential Medal of Honor, n.d., <http://www.whitehouse.gov/news/releases/2005/11/20051109-10.html> (September 15, 2008).

30. "Grand opening for new Ali centre," *BBC Sport* webpage, n.d., <http://news.bbc.co.uk/sport2/hi/boxing/4455412.stm> (September 10, 2008).

31. The Muhammad Ali Center webpage, <http://www.alicenter.org/Pages/default.aspx> (September 10, 2008).

32. Dave Perkins, "In Louisville, they adore Muhammad Ali," *Toronto Star*, September 18, 2008, <http://www.thestar.com/Sports/Golf/article/501564> (September 20, 2008).

33. Paul Mahoney, "Faldo overwhelmed by meeting with Ali, while Azinger was overjoyed," n.d., <http://www.golf.com> (September 20, 2008).

34. Muhammad Ali with Hana Yasmeen Ali, p. 209.

Chapter 10. Living Legacy

1. Thomas Hauser, *Muhammad Ali: His Life and Times* (New York: Simon & Schuster, 1991), p. 447.

2. Ibid., p. 458.

3. Kleran Mulvaney, "How we picked the 50 greatest fighters," *ESPN*, <http://sports.espn.go.com/sports/boxing/greatest/news/story?id=2815643> (January 16, 2009).

4. Hauser, p. 454.

5. Ibid., p. 327.

6. Ibid., p. 452.

7. Ibid., p. 508.

8. Muhammad Ali with Hana Yasmeen Ali, *The Soul of a Butterfly: Reflections on Life's Journey* (New York: Simon & Schuster, 2004), p. 205.

Further Reading

Books

Ali, Muhammad, with Hana Yasmeen Ali. *The Soul of a Butterfly: Reflections on Life's Journey*. New York: Simon and Schuster, 2004.

Ali, Muhammad, with Richard Durham. *The Greatest*. New York: Random House, 1976.

Brunt, Stephen. *Facing Ali*. Guilford, Conn.: The Lyons Press, 2002.

Dennis, Felix, and Don Atyeo. *Muhammad Ali: The Glory Years*. New York: Hyperion, 2003.

Simpson, Paul. *The Rough Guide to Muhammad Ali*. London: Rough Guides, 2004.

Smith, Charles R., Jr., *Twelve Rounds to Glory: The Story of Muhammad Ali*. Cambridge, Mass.: Candlewick Press, 2007.

Torres, Jose, and Bert Randolph Sugar. *Sting Like a Bee: The Muhammad Ali Story*. New York: Contemporary Books, 2002.

Internet Addresses

Muhammad Ali Center
<http://www.alicenter.org/Pages/default.aspx>

The Official Muhammad Ali Web Site
<http://www.ali.com/>

Index